The ESSE

MW00453901

BASIC

Jerry R. Shipman, Ph.D.
Chairperson of Mathematics Department
Alabama Agricultural and Mechanical University
Normal, Alabama

Research and Education Association
61 Ethel Road West
Piscataway, New Jersey 08854

THE ESSENTIALS® OF BASIC

Copyright © 1989 by Research and Education Association. All rights reserved. No part of this book may be reproduced in any form without permission of the publisher.

Printed in the United States of America

Library of Congress Catalog Card Number 89-61499

International Standard Book Number 0–87891–684-9

Revised Printing, 1992

ESSENTIALS is a registered trademark of Research and Education Association, Piscataway, New Jersey

WHAT "THE ESSENTIALS" WILL DO FOR YOU

This book is a review and study guide. It is comprehensive and it is concise.

It helps in preparing for exams, in doing homework, and remains a handy reference source at all times.

It condenses the vast amount of detail characteristic of the subject matter and summarizes the **essentials** of the field.

It will thus save hours of study and preparation time.

The book provides quick access to the important facts, principles, theorems, concepts, and equations in the field.

Materials needed for exams can be reviewed in summary form – eliminating the need to read and re-read many pages of textbook and class notes. The summaries will even tend to bring detail to mind that had been previously read or noted.

This "ESSENTIALS" book has been prepared by an expert in the field, and has been carefully reviewed to assure accuracy and maximum usefulness.

Dr. Max Fogiel
Program Director

CONTENTS

PART I: MINIMAL BASIC

CHAPTER 1

FUNDAMENTALS OF BASIC

1.1   ELEMENTS OF BASIC

Minimal BASIC is a subset of the BASIC (Beginner's All-purpose Symbolic Instruction Code) language that is compatible with the standard proposed by the American National Standards Institute (ANSI). The BASIC language is structured around a set of nine elements briefly described as follows:

Character Set—The proposed ANSI Standard defines 60 characters. They are:

(1)   The 26 alpha characters in the letters of the alphabet.

(2)   The 10 numeric characters given by the digits 0, 1, 2, 3, 4, 5, 6, 7, 8, and 9.

1

(3)   The 24 ANSI standard special characters of the various special characters which appear on a computer keyboard. These 24 characters are described in Table 1.1.1.

TABLE 1.1.1   TWENTY-FOUR ANSI SPECIAL CHARACTERS

Character	Description	Character	Description
	space or blank	!	exclamation point
"	quote	#	number sign
$	dollar	%	percent
&	ampersand	'	apostrophe
(	open parenthesis	)	closed parenthesis
*	asterisk	+	plus
−	minus/dash	/	slant
.	period	,	comma
:	colon	;	semicolon
<	less than	>	greater than
=	equals	?	question mark
^	circumflex	_	underline

Strings—A string is any sequence of characters. For example, quoted strings, such as "ESSENTIALS OF BASIC" and "TOTAL = $", are used in BASIC.

Numbers—A number or numeric value in BASIC can be an integer (a number without a decimal), a real (a number with a decimal point) or an exponential (a number expressed in scientific or E-notation).

Constants and Variables—In BASIC a symbol name is called a variable. A constant represents a fixed value in the program. Constants and variables are used to represent numeric and non-numeric data within the program. For example, E, S, and T represent numeric variables and 40, 20, and 900 are numeric constants.

Key Words—Certain words in BASIC are called key words because they either describe particular operations to be performed or communicate certain information to the computer. For example, LET, PRINT, and END are key words in BASIC.

Functions—Certain operations in BASIC are performed by using BASIC-supplied functions. For example, the SQR function is used to take a square root and the ABS function is used to find the absolute value.

Expressions—An expression is a combination of one or more variables, constants, functions, and special characters. For example, 5 * A + 35 is an arithmetic expression.

Statements—A BASIC statement or instruction either directs the computer to perform a specific task or declares certain information which the computer needs. BASIC statements are combinations of characters, strings, numbers, variables, key words, constants, functions, and expressions.

Line Numbers—A line number is a unique one- to five-digit number that must precede each BASIC statement in a program. It must not contain a leading sign, embedded spaces, commas, decimal points or any other punctuation. Line numbers are used to:

(1)   Indicate the sequence of statement execution,

(2)   Provide control points for branching, and

(3)   Add, change and delete statement.

In Program 1.2 below (See Section 1.2), the numbers 10, 20, and 30 are line numbers. The system command RUN does not have a line number.

> **Line Number Rule 1:** BASIC statements have line numbers, and system commands don't.

1.2 GENERAL CHARACTERISTICS OF A BASIC PROGRAM

A BASIC program is generally composed of:

(1) A sequence of statements, each with a line number.

(2) The last statement in the sequence contains the END statement.

For example, the following short BASIC program (1.2) has three statements. The first one instructs the system to compute the value of A, the second displays the results of A on an output device (e.g., monitor), and the third statement stops or terminates the run or execution of the program. The system command RUN causes this program to be executed.

PROGRAM 1.2   EXAMPLE OF A SHORT BASIC PROGRAM

BASIC Program	10 LET A = 0.25 * (200 - 75) 20 PRINT A 30 END
System Command	RUN

Displayed Result	31.25

1.3 SOME BASIC SYSTEM COMMANDS

Two types of instructions are used with BASIC computer systems. One type represents the BASIC statements, such as the LET statement, the PRINT statement, etc. The second type represents the system commands associated with the BASIC system. A summary of some common system commands found with BASIC systems is shown in Table 1.3.1.

TABLE 1.3.1   SUMMARY OF SOME COMMON SYSTEM COM-
MANDS USED WITH BASIC SYSTEMS

System Command	Function
RUN	Causes the BASIC program currently in main storage to be executed.
LIST	Causes all or part of the BASIC program currently in main storage to be displayed.
NEW	Causes deletion of the BASIC program currently in main storage and indicates the start of a new program to be created in main storage.
CLS or HOME	Erases all the information on the monitor's screen and places the cursor in the upper left corner of the screen.

SAVE filename or
SAVE "filename"   Saves or files the current program into
                         auxiliary storage for later use.

LOAD filename or
LOAD "filename"   Loads a previously stored program from
                         auxiliary storage into main storage.

1.4   VARIABLES AND CONSTANTS

A variable is a symbol that identifies a location in the computer's memory where a particular value (data item) is stored (found).

1.4.1   TYPES OF VARIABLES

In BASIC variables are classified as either numeric or string variables.

Numeric Variables—Variables that store numeric values are called numeric variables. For example, the numeric values 25.5 and - 2.3 can be stored under the numeric variables B and G, respectively. Numeric variables are classified as simple or subscripted. Simple numeric variables store single numeric values whereas subscripted numeric variables store multiple numeric values.

> **Variable Rule 1:** BASIC does not allow special characters such as a / or % to be used in forming variable names.

String Variables—Variables that store strings and are named by using a letter followed by a dollar sign are called string variables. For example B$, D$, and T$ all represent string variables. As is true of numeric variables, string variables can be classified as simple string variables, those that store a single string, and subscripted string variables, those that store multiple strings.

Variable Rule 2: In BASIC a string variable name must end with a dollar sign.

1.4.2 TYPES OF CONSTANTS

In BASIC constants are classified as either numeric or string constants.

Numeric Constants—A numeric constant is a decimal representation of a number (integer, real or in scientific notation or E-notation).

Constant Rule 1: Commas and other special characters are not permissible within a numeric constant.

Constant Rule 2: The maximum number of digits in a numeric constant differ from computer system to computer system.

Constant Rule 3: The maximum value allowed for a number in E-notation differs from system to system.

String Constants—A string constant consists of a string enclosed in quotations; its value is the string of characters between the quotations.

> **Constant Rule 4:** The maximum number of characters (length) that can be included in a string varies from one version of BASIC to another.

All BASIC systems allow variable names to be one or two characters in length where the first one must by an alphabetic character.

1.5   END STATEMENT

The END statement instructs the system to stop executing the program. It is used to: (1) mark the physical end of a program and (2) terminate the execution of the program. The general structure of the END statement and an example are given in Table 1.5.1 as follows:

TABLE 1.5.1   THE END STATEMENT

General
Structure: line no. END

Example: 30 END (See Program 1.2)

1.6   LET STATEMENT

A LET statement is used (1) to perform and store calculations, (2) to assign a constant to a storage location, or (3) to copy the contents of one storage location into another. In Program 1.2 the statement:

$$10 \text{ LET A} = 0.25 * (200 - 75)$$

is an example of a LET statement in which the value 31.25 is stored in location A. The variable in a LET statement may also be a string variable such as the statement:

20 LET B$ = "BASIC IS OK"

On most systems BASIC will accept a LET statement without the use of the word LET in the statement. The structure of the LET statement and some additional examples are shown in Table 1.6.1.

TABLE 1.6.1   THE LET STATEMENT

General
Structure: line no. LET variable = expression or
                   line no. LET string variable = "expression"

         or

                   line no. variable = expression or
                   line no. string variable = "expression"

Examples:

Type	**Illustration**
LET variable = constant	Ex. 1: 10 LET B = 15.5
LET variable = variable	Ex. 2: 20 LET C = F
LET variable = combination of	Ex. 3: 30 K = 2 * C − 4/B
constants and variables	Ex. 4: 35 LET F(I) = C(J) + J
separated by operation	
symbols	
LET string var = "expression"	Ex. 5: 40 LET R$ ="Total= $"
	Ex. 6: 50 A$ = R$+ "1000.00"

LET Statement Rule 1: The equal sign (=) in a LET statement dictates that the storage content of the variable to the left of the equal sign is to be replaced by the value of the expression to the right of the equal sign.

LET Statement Rule 2: If the expression in a LET statement contains two or more different operations, then (1) all exponentations are performed first; (2) all multiplications and divisions are performed next; and (3) all additions and subtractions are performed last. This is referred to as the arithmetic hierarchy rule.

LET Statement Rule 3: If the expression in a LET statement involves two or more operations, then the computation results will be performed consistent with a left-to-right scan of the expression by the computer. This is called the left-to-right rule.

LET Statement Rule 4: If the expression in a LET statement contains two or more arithmetic operations, then BASIC applies the so-called left-to-right rule and the arithmetic hierarchy rule in performing the operations.

LET Statement Rule 5: When parentheses are inserted into a LET expression, the part of the expression within the parentheses is evaluated first by the LET Statement Rules 2 and 3 and then the remaining expression is also evaluated according to the same rules.

> **LET Statement Rule 6:** Every variable appearing to the right of the equal sign in a LET statement should have been previously defined in the program.

1.7   PRINT STATEMENT

The PRINT statement is used to output (1) numeric constants, (2) values of numeric expressions, (3) values of variables (the contents of computer memory locations), and (4) string constants (labels, captions or column headings, other textual matter, report headings, etc.) via a display device, such as a monitor or printer.

Table 1.7.1 gives the general structure of the PRINT statement and some examples.

TABLE 1.7.1   THE PRINT STATEMENT

General
Structure: line no. PRINT list

where "list" refers to:

(1) A numerical or string constant,
(2) A numerical or string variable,
(3) An arithmetic expression, or
(4) A combination of constants, variables, and expressions separated by commas and/ or semicolons.

NOTE: Expressions of string constants and string variables are enclosed in quotation marks.

Examples:

Ex. 1: 10 PRINT
Ex. 2: 20 PRINT A
Ex. 3: 30 PRINT A, B, (A + B)/2
Ex. 4: 40 PRINT A, B; C; A$
Ex. 5: 50 PRINT "The Total is "; T
Ex. 6: 60 PRINT "Area = "; A, "L = "; L, "W = "; W
Ex. 7: 70 PRINT 25.4, "R = 25% ";

1.7.1   PRINTING ZONES

Output on a print line is divided into print zones. The number and width of print zones varies slightly from system to system. The use of commas to separate the elements in the print list automatically executes the printing of the elements in particular zones. If a print line exceeds the number of characters for a print zone on a system, the printing continues on into the next zone. The normal zones for a 40-column line are three — columns 1-16, zone 1; columns 17-31, zone 2; and, columns 32-40, zone 3.

1.7.2   OUTPUT SPACING

Variations in the use of the PRINT statement allow for better control of spacing of printed output. Uses of the comma and semicolon affect spacing in BASIC output as follows:

(A)   When a comma is used to separate items in a PRINT list, it has the effect of moving the print element on the display device to the next zone leaving blank spaces in the current zone.

(B)   When a semicolon is used to separate items in a print list, it has the effect of "packing" the zones. Packed

12

zones mean that there are zero blank spaces between output information.

(C) A comma or semicolon at the end of the list in a PRINT statement (called a trailing **comma** or **semicolon**), tells the display device to suppress the carriage return and line feed operations and continue to print subsequent information on the same print line.

(D) A PRINT statement without a list yields a blank line on which nothing is "printed." See example in Table 1.7.1.

Output Rule 1: Every variable appearing in an output statement should have been previously defined in the program.

1.8 REM STATEMENT

The REMark statement is used to describe or document programs. This statement, unlike other BASIC statements, is non-executable. The general structure of the statement and some examples are given in Table 1.8.1.

TABLE 1.8.1   THE REM STATEMENT

General
Structure: line no. REM unquoted string

Examples:

Ex. 1:   10 REM J. R. Shipman
Ex. 2:   20 REM THE ESSENTIALS OF BASIC
Ex. 3:   30 REM *****PROGRAM 1.2*****

1.9 DEMONSTRATION PROGRAM

```
100 REM * ** PROGRAM: CALCULATION OF GAS
101 REM        MILEAGE OF A CAR* **
110 REM D = Distance Traveled in Miles
112 REM G = Gasoline Used in Gallons
115 REM M = Mileage in Miles/Gallon
120 LET D = 300
122 LET G = 15
124 LET B$ = "JOHN WOE'S CAR AVERAGED …"
126 LET C$ = "MILES/GALLON OF GAS."
130 LET M = D/G
135 PRINT "DISTANCE", "GASOLINE", "MILEAGE"
140 PRINT "TRAVELED", "USED", "PER/GAL"
145 PRINT
150 PRINT D, G, M
160 PRINT
165 PRINT
170 PRINT B$; M; C$
200 END
```

Lines 100-115 describe the program and document the variables. Lines 120-126 are assignment statements for the real numeric and string variables. Line 130 calculates the mileage and stores the results. Lines 135-145 print headings and skip a single line. Lines 150-165 print the values of the real numeric variables and skip two single lines. Line 170 prints the values of two string variables and one real numeric variable. Line 200 is the end of the program.

CHAPTER 2

INPUT AND OUTPUT STATEMENTS

2.1 INPUT STATEMENT

The INPUT statement allows the user to supply data to the program while the program is executing or running. In other words, when the program is executed the INPUT statement prints a question mark (?) on an output device to remind the user to enter numeric or string data for the program via an input device, such as a keyboard. The INPUT statement facilitates interactive programming. The general structure of the INPUT statement and some examples are given in Table 2.1.1.

TABLE 2.1.1   THE INPUT STATEMENT

General
Structure: line no. INPUT variable, ..., variable

or

line no. INPUT "input prompt message"; variable, ..., variable

Examples:

| | |
| Input Statements | **Example of data
from an external source** |

Input Statements	Example of data from an external source
Ex. 1: 10 INPUT Z	- 2.5
Ex. 2: 20 INPUT A, B	3,4
Ex. 3: 30 INPUT A$, C	BASIC, 1988
Ex. 4: 40 INPUT "ENTER Y OR N"; A$	Y

INPUT Rule 1: Every variable appearing in the program whose value is directly obtained through input must be listed in an INPUT statement before it is used elsewhere in the program.

INPUT Rule 2: Numeric data assigned to numeric variables through the use of the INPUT statement must take the form of numeric constants.

2.2 READ AND DATA STATEMENTS
2.2.1 DATA STATEMENT

The DATA statement provides for the creation of a sequence of data items for use by the READ statement. The DATA statement consists of the keyword DATA followed by a list of data items separated by mandatory commas. The data items may be numeric or string. The general structure of the DATA statement and some examples are given below in Table 2.2.1.

TABLE 2.2.1   THE DATA STATEMENT

General
Structure: line no. DATA data item, ..., data item

16

Examples (with READ statements):

Ex. 1:   100 DATA 2, –5.5, 0.25, –70
Ex. 2:   110 READ A, B1, C, D2

— — — — — — — — — — — —

Ex. 3:   120 DATA 0, –1.2E12, 17.245
Ex. 4:   130 READ A1, E, F(J)

— — — — — — — — — — — —

Ex. 5:   140 DATA 20, "CENTS", "$ ", 25, "NO: ", "2.45"
Ex. 6:   150 READ G, B$, C$, H, A$, H$

DATA Rule 1: Numeric data items placed in a DATA statement must be formulated as numeric constants.

DATA Rule 2: String data items placed in a DATA statement may be formulated with or without surrounding quotation marks, provided the string contains no trailing or leading blanks or embedded commas or semicolons. If the string contains a trailing or leading blank or an embedded comma or semicolon, it must be surrounded with quotation marks.

DATA Rule 3: The DATA statement may be located anywhere before the end line in a program.

Data items from all of the DATA statements in a BASIC program are arranged in the main storage area in the computer into a single data sequence holding area. The ordering of the data items is based on:

(1)   The ascending line numbers of the DATA statements and

17

(2)   The order from left to right of the data items within each DATA statement.

The DATA statement is a non-executable statement.

2.2.2   READ STATEMENT

The READ statement provides for the assignment of values to variables from a sequence of data items created from DATA statements. The READ statement causes the variables in its list to be assigned specific values, in order, from the data sequence formed by all of the DATA statements. The general structure of the READ statement and some examples are given in Table 2.2.1 and Table 2.2.2.

TABLE 2.2.2   THE READ STATEMENT

General
Structure: line no. READ variable, ..., variable

(The variables in the list may either be numeric or string variables or a combination separated by commas.)

Examples:

Ex. 1:   150 READ Z$, A
Ex. 2:   175 READ B$(J)
Ex. 3:   250 DATA "FALSE", −10, "NEED WORK"

Also, see Table 2.2.1

READ Rule 1: Every variable appearing in the program whose value is directly obtained by a READ should be listed in a READ statement before it is used elsewhere in the program.

> **READ Rule 2:** A program containing a READ statement must also have at least one DATA statement with a value to be assigned to each variable listed in the READ statement.

> **READ Rule 3:** Numeric variables in READ statements require numeric constants as data items in DATA statements, and string variables require quoted strings or unquoted strings as data. The READ variables must be in the same sequence as the data items in the DATA statements.

To visualize the relationship between the READ statement and its associated DATA statement, think of a pointer associated with the data sequence holding area. When the program is first executed, this pointer points to the first data item in the data sequence. Each time a READ statement is executed, the variables in the list are assigned specific values from the data sequence and the pointer appropriately advances one value per variable.

2.3 THE RESTORE STATEMENT

The RESTORE statement allows the data in DATA statements in a given program to be reread as often as desired by the same or other READ statements in the program. The general structure of the RESTORE statement is given with an example in Table 2.3.1.

TABLE 2.3.1   THE RESTORE STATEMENT

General
Structure: line no. RESTORE

Example: 100 RESTORE

Note: In general, systems which use Microsoft BASIC may optionally allow a line number to follow the keyword RESTORE. When this occurs the data pointer in the system is reset to the first data item in the DATA statement with that line number.

2.4   THE TAB FUNCTION

In order to create more attractive output with the use of the comma and semicolon in the PRINT statement, the TAB function is available. The TAB function is a formatting feature which allows more exact spacing in an output. The function can only be used with the PRINT statement. Its general structure is given with examples in Table 2.4.1.

TABLE 2.4.1   THE TAB FUNCTION

General
Structure: line no. PRINT TAB (expression)

(The expression or the argument may be a numeric constant, variable, arithmetic expression, or function reference.)

Examples:

Ex. 1:   10 PRINT TAB (10); A; "BASIC"
Ex. 2:   20 PRINT B; TAB (17); 25
Ex. 3:   25 C = 32
Ex. 4:   30 PRINT C$; TAB (C); D

The value of the expression or argument determines the position on the line of the next character to be displayed, relative to the starting position of the line.

2.5 SOME COMMON ERRORS

Some of the common input and read errors are as follows:

(A) Too few values entered for the variables in the INPUT statement or too few data blocks for the READ statement. In the case of the READ statement, the error will cause the BASIC system to print an "out of data" execution error message.

(B) Mismatching by type of variables and values in the INPUT and READ statements.

(C) Omission of quotes around a string constant containing an embedded comma when entering data in the INPUT statement or reading data items for the READ statement.

(D) Placement of a comma at the end of a data line in a DATA statement.

(E) Incorrect sequencing of INPUT, READ and PRINT statements in a program.

2.6 DEMONSTRATION PROGRAMS

```
100 REM **VOLUME OF A CUBE **
110 INPUT"ENTER Length, Width, Depth"; L, W, D
115 V = L * W * D
```

```
117 PRINT
120 PRINT "LENGTH", "WIDTH", "DEPTH"
125 PRINT L, W, D
127 PRINT
130 PRINT "THE VOLUME OF THE CUBE IS "; V
150 END
```

Line 100 describes the program. Line 110 prints a prompt and accepts input values for the three variables. Line 115 calculates the volume. Lines 117-127 skip a single line, print headings, print the values of the variables, and skip a single line. Line 130 prints a label and the value of the volume. Line 150 is the end of the program.

```
200 REM ** AREA AND PERIMETER OF A RECTANGLE **
202 REM   L=LENGTH, W=WIDTH, A=AREA, AND
203 REM   P=PERIMETER
204 LET B = 5
205 READ F$, L, W
210 LET A = L * W
212 PRINT TAB(13); "LENGTH"; TAB(B); "WIDTH"
215 PRINT F$; " 1"; TAB(B); L; TAB(B); W
217 PRINT
220 PRINT "AREA OF FIGURE 1 IS "; A
225 RESTORE
230 READ F$, L, W
235 PRINT
240 P = 2 * L + 2 * W
250 PRINT "PERIMETER OF FIGURE 1 IS "; P
255 DATA "FIGURE", 10.5, 4
300 END
```

Lines 200-204 describe the program, document the variables and assign a value to B. Line 205 reads values from the DATA statement. Lines 210-220 calculate the area, print headings with tabulation, print values of the variables with tabulation, skip a single line, and print a label with the value of the area. Line 225 restores the DATA statement. Line 230 reads values from the DATA statement. Lines 235-250 skip a single line, calculate the perimeter and print a label with the value of the perimeter. Line 255 is not executed and line 300 is the end of the program.

CHAPTER 3

INTRODUCTION TO CONTROL STATEMENTS

3.1 GOTO STATEMENT

The GOTO statement is a control statement, since it causes the computer to interrupt the normal sequential execution of a BASIC program, and branch to some other executable instruction in the program that is not the next instruction in the normal sequence. This interrupt in the normal flow of a program is referred to as **transfer of control** or **branching**. The general structure of the GOTO statement and some examples are given in Table 3.1.1.

TABLE 3.1.1   THE GOTO STATEMENT

General
Structure: line no. GOTO line number

Examples:

Ex. 1:   50 GOTO 100
Ex. 2:   75 GOTO 30
Ex. 3:   99 GOTO 500

Consider the first example in Table 3.1.1, that is, the statement 50 GOTO 100. When statement 50 is executed, the computer interrupts the sequential execution of the program and the transfer of control goes to the statement labeled with line number 100 — the next statement to be executed. The GOTO statement is also called an **unconditional branch statement.**

The GOTO statement can be used to transfer computer control to any statement in a BASIC program even though the statement has a lower or higher line number than the line number for the GOTO statement. If the GOTO statement sends the control to a higher line number in the program, then the line numbers between the GOTO statement and the higher line number will be skipped and thus not executed.

3.2   IF/THEN STATEMENT

The IF/THEN statement requires the computer to test a condition and then, based on whether the condition is true or false, to take a proper transfer of control action. Such a statement is required in BASIC programming if one is to solve problems that involve decision-making algorithms.

The IF/THEN statement is also useful to perform loops in a program for algorithms involving repetitive operations and to determine when to terminate a looping process. A loop may have a decision concerning termination at its top or bottom. A loop that has the termination decision at the top of the loop is called a **Do-While structure.** On the other hand, a loop that has the termination decision at the bottom of the loop is called a **Do-Until structure.**

The general BASIC structure of the IF/THEN statement and some examples are given in Table 3.2.1

TABLE 3.2.1   THE IF/THEN STATEMENT

General
Structure: (1)   line no. IF condition THEN line number
             or
             (2)   line no. IF condition THEN statement

Examples: For structure (1)

Ex. 1:   100 IF X < 0 THEN 400
Ex. 2:   120 IF X + 2 >= 6   THEN 550
Ex. 3:   150 IF T$ <> "NO" THEN 700
         400 . . .

         For structure (2)

Ex. 4:   175 IF Y − 5 > F/2 THEN A = A + 1
Ex. 5:   180 IF C + A <= Y THEN C = 2 * Y
Ex. 6:   200 IF R$ = "YES" THEN PRINT R$

In Table 3.2.1 the condition between the keywords IF and THEN specifies a comparative relationship between expressions that is either true or false. The condition is made up of at least two expressions and a relational or logical operator. The expressions may be associated with either numeric or string values. The six relational operators used in a condition are indicated in Table 3.2.2. The logical operators are covered later in this section. Examples of the use of the relational operators in IF/THEN statements are given in Table 3.2.1.

If the condition between the keywords IF and THEN is true and a line number follows the keyword THEN, control transfers to the stated line number. However, if a statement follows the keyword THEN, the statement is executed and the computer continues with the next sequential statement in the program.

If the condition between the keywords IF and THEN is false and a line number or a statement follows the keyword THEN, the line number or the statement after the keyword THEN is ignored and the next sequential statement following the IF/THEN statement in the program is executed.

TABLE 3.2.2 RELATIONAL OPERATORS USED IN CONDITIONS

Relation	Relational Operator Symbol in BASIC
Equal to	=
Greater than	>
Greater than or equal to	>=
Less than	<
Less than or equal to	<=
Not equal to	<>

The logic flow for the IF/THEN statement using the Do-While structure and Do-Until structure, respectively, is shown in Figure 3.2.1.

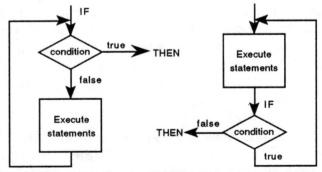

FIGURE 3.2.1—Logic Flow for IF/THEN Statement in Do-While and Do-Until Structures.

27

An example of the Do-While structure in a segment of a BASIC program is shown in Table 3.2.3. Notice that the IF/THEN statement is at the top of the looping process, while the GOTO statement, a significant part of this structure, is at the bottom.

An example of the Do-Until structure in a segment of a BASIC program is shown in Table 3.2.4. Notice that the IF/THEN statement only occurs at the bottom of the looping process.

TABLE 3.2.3: EXAMPLE OF DO-WHILE STRUCTURE IN BASIC

```
10 LET S = 0
20 LET I = 1
30 IF I > 100 THEN 90
40      LET S = S + I
50      LET I = I + 1
60 GOTO 30
90 PRINT "SUM= "; S
```

TABLE 3.2.4   EXAMPLE OF DO-UNTIL STRUCTURE IN BASIC

```
10 LET S = 0
20 LET I = 1
30      LET S = S + I
40      LET I = I + 1
50 IF I < 100 THEN 30
90 PRINT "SUM = "; S
```

3.2.1 THE IF/THEN/ELSE STATEMENT

A second type of IF/THEN statement is the IF/THEN/ELSE statement. The general BASIC structure and some examples of this statement are given in Table 3.2.5.

TABLE 3.2.5   THE IF/THEN/ELSE STATEMENT

General
Structure: line no. IF condition THEN line no. or statement
                        ELSE line no. or statement

Examples:

Ex. 1:   100 IF A < 5 THEN 200 ELSE 900
Ex. 2:   150 IF X > Y THEN LET A = 5 ELSE LET X = X * Y
Ex. 3:   200 IF A > 5 THEN PRINT A ELSE PRINT Y
          900 . . .

Caution: This statement is not available on the Apple.

The IF/THEN/ELSE statement is very similar to the IF/THEN statement. The important difference occurs between the IF/THEN/ELSE statement and IF/THEN statement, which transfers the computer control to the next line number in the program as a result of a false condition between the keywords IF and THEN. If the condition is false in an IF/THEN/ELSE statement then the computer control transfers to the line number or statement after the keyword ELSE. In the case where a line number follows the THEN or ELSE keyword, then the computer control transfers to that line number. On the other hand, if a non-transfer statement follows these keywords, then the statements are executed and the next line number after the IF/THEN/ELSE is executed.

Notice that the relational operators are used with both of the IF/THEN and IF/THEN/ELSE statements. The other set of operators, namely logical operators, can also be used with these statements. The logical operators, along with examples of their uses in BASIC, are shown in Table 3.2.6.

TABLE 3.2.6 LOGICAL OPERATORS AND EXAMPLES IN BASIC

Relation	Basic Logical Operators
Conjunction	AND
Disjunction	OR
Negation	NOT

Examples: (IF/THEN statements)

Ex. 1: 100 IF Q$ = "R" AND B < 10 THEN 300
Ex. 2: 250 IF X > Y OR A=B AND F < 3 OR NOT H=R THEN PRINT R$

(IF/THEN/ELSE statements)

Ex. 3: 100 IF X=Y AND A=B THEN PRINT Y ELSE GOTO 500
Ex. 4: 200 IF X < Y OR T > 9 THEN LET X=T ELSE PRINT T
Ex. 5: 300 IF N$ = "BASIC" AND A`< B THEN 150 ELSE 250

The logic flow of the IF/THEN/ELSE statement is shown in Figure 3.2.2.

Based on the fundamentals of logic and BASIC, decisions for the execution of IF/THEN and IF/THEN/ELSE statements using each of the three logical operators are considered as follows.

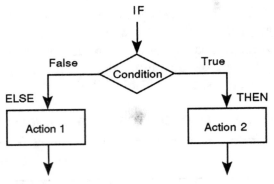

FIGURE 3.2.2—IF/THEN/ELSE Logic Structure

3.2.2 THE LOGICAL OPERATOR: AND

Consider the case of a general IF/THEN statement using the AND operator:

> line no. IF <condition A> AND <condition B> THEN <action>

If each condition is true, then the compound condition A and B is true and the Action part of the statement is executed. If either of the conditions if false, then the compound condition A and B is false and control transfers to the next sequential statement in the program.

Consider the case of a general IF/THEN/ELSE statement using the AND operator:

> line no. IF <cond A> AND <cond B> THEN <act 1> ELSE <act 2>

As indicated above, if each condition is true, then the compound condition A and B is true and control transfers to Action 1. Otherwise, if the compound condition is false (that is, one or both of the conditions being false), then control transfers to

Action 2 rather than Action 1 in the statement.

> **Logical Operator Rule 1:** The logical operator AND requires that all conditions be true for the compound condition to be true.

3.2.3   THE LOGICAL OPERATOR: OR

Consider the case of a general IF/THEN statement using the OR operator:

> line no. IF <condition A> OR <condition B> THEN <action 1>

If either one of the conditions or both conditions are true, then the compound OR condition A and B is true, and the control transfers to Action 1. Otherwise, control transfers to the next sequential statement in the program.

Consider the case of a general IF/THEN/ELSE statement using the OR operator:

> line no. IF <cond A> OR <cond B> THEN <act 1> ELSE <act 2>

If either one of the conditions or both conditions are true, then the compound OR condition is true, and the control transfers to Action 1. Otherwise, control transfers to Action 2 rather than Action 1 in the statement.

> **Logical Operator Rule 2:** The logical operator OR requires that one or both of the conditions be true for the compound condition to be true.

3.2.4   THE LOGICAL OPERATOR: NOT

Consider the case of a general IF/THEN statement using the NOT logical operator:

> line no. IF NOT <condition A> THEN <action 1>

If the NOT form of condition A is true, then Action 1 will be executed, otherwise, the next sequential statement in the program will be executed.

Consider the case of a general IF/THEN/ELSE statement using the NOT logical operator:

> line no. IF NOT <cond A> THEN <act 1> ELSE <act 2>

If the NOT form of condition A is true, then Action 1 will only be executed. If the NOT form of condition A is false, then Action 2 will be executed.

> **Logical Operator Rule 3:** The logical operator NOT requires that the relational expression be false for the condition to be true. If the relational expression is true, then the condition is false.

If parentheses are used with the logical operators in the IF/THEN and IF/THEN/ELSE statements, respectively, then the evaluation of the compound conditions are controlled by the parentheses. If no parentheses are used with the logical operators in the IF/THEN and IF/THEN/ELSE statements, respectively, then the computer evaluates the compound condition in accordance with the rules of precedence.

Like the IF/THEN statement, a useful function of the IF/THEN/ELSE statement in a program is to perform an "End to the File" test to determine whether to terminate a looping process.

3.3 THE WHILE/WEND STATEMENTS

The WHILE and WEND statements in BASIC represent another method for controlling a looping process. These statements can be used to implement the Do-While structure, but are not available for the Apple. The general BASIC structure and some examples of the WHILE and WEND statements are given in Table 3.3.1 and Table 3.3.2, respectively.

TABLE 3.3.1   THE WHILE STATEMENT

General
Structure: line no. WHILE <condition>

Examples:

Ex. 1:   100 WHILE A = 0
Ex. 2:   150 WHILE A$ <> "SUM"
Ex. 3:   200 WHILE A > B * C − D * A

Caution: This statement is not available for the Apple.

TABLE 3.3.2   THE WEND STATEMENT

General
Structure: line no. WEND

Examples:

Ex. 1:   500 WEND
Ex. 2:   900 WEND

Caution: This statement is not available for the Apple.

An illustration of the WHILE/WEND looping process in BASIC is shown in Table 3.3.3.

TABLE 3.3.3: ILLUSTRATION OF WHILE/WEND LOOP

```
loop        10 LET S = 0
            20 LET I = 1
            30 WHILE I <= 100
            40      LET S = S + I
            50      LET I = I + 1
            60 WEND
            90 PRINT "SUM= ";  S
```

WHILE Rule 1: The WHILE statement may be located anywhere in the program before the corresponding WEND statement.

WEND Rule 1: The WEND statement may be located anywhere in the program after the corresponding WHILE statement and before the END statement.

WHILE/WEND Rule 1: The WHILE and WEND statement may be used in nested format.

3.4 FOR/NEXT LOOPS

The computer can repeat a group of instructions over and over again within a program, without running the program each time there is new data. This process, as indicated in the previous section, is referred to as **looping**. The FOR and NEXT statements, commonly called the FOR/NEXT loop, work together to make it possible in BASIC to execute looping in a program. Conceptually the loop operates as shown in Figure 3.4.1.

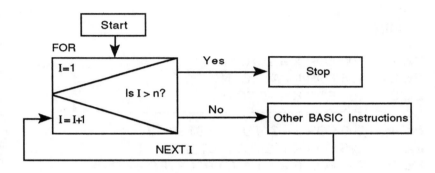

FIGURE 3.4.1—Conceptual View of FOR/NEXT Loop

3.4.1 "FOR" STATEMENT

The FOR statement indicates the beginning of a loop in a program, whereas the NEXT statement represents the end or foot of the loop. All executable instructions between the FOR and NEXT represent the body of the loop. The general structure and some examples of the FOR statement are given in Table 3.4.1.

TABLE 3.4.1   THE FOR STATEMENT

General
Structure: line no. FOR k=initial value TO limit value
              or
              line no. FOR k=initial value TO limit value
                      STEP increment value

36

(The k represents a simple numeric variable called the control or index variable. The initial, limit and increment values are each expressions.)

(The absence of the keyword STEP in the FOR statement means that the increment value is 1.)

Examples:

Ex. 1:   100 FOR X = 1 TO 10
Ex. 2:   125 FOR I = A   TO N
Ex. 3:   150 FOR K = –5 TO 0.2
———————————————
Ex. 4:   200 FOR J = 2 TO –10 STEP –2
Ex. 5:   225 FOR K = G TO R STEP C
Ex. 6:   250 FOR F = A + 1 TO R/K STEP 2 * B

FOR Rule 1: The FOR statement may be located anywhere in a program before the corresponding NEXT statement.

FOR Rule 2: The value of the increment value in the FOR statement must not be zero.

FOR Rule 3: Each FOR statement must have a corresponding NEXT statement with the same control or index variable.

FOR Rule 4: The initial, limit and incremental values of the FOR statement can be either a numeric constant, numeric variable, or arithmetic expression.

> **FOR Rule 5:** The control or index variable can be utilized within the body of the loop.

3.4.2 "NEXT" STATEMENT

The NEXT statement defines the end of the FOR/NEXT loop. The general structure and some examples of the NEXT statement are given in Table 3.4.2 below.

TABLE 3.4.2   THE NEXT STATEMENT

General
Structure: line no. NEXT k (control or index variable)

Examples:

Ex. 1:   110 NEXT X
Ex. 2:   130 NEXT J
Ex. 3:   275 NEXT F

> **NEXT Rule 1:** The NEXT statement must have a higher line number than its corresponding FOR statement.

Keep in mind the following rules concerning FOR/NEXT loops.

> **FOR/NEXT Rule 1:** Branching out of a FOR/NEXT loop other than at the foot of the loop (the NEXT statement) is permissible but is generally discouraged.

FOR/NEXT Rule 2: Branching into the body of a FOR/NEXT loop from outside the loop is either not permitted by the computer system or not advisable in a program.

FOR/NEXT RULE 3: Depending on the computer system, the value of the control or index variable may not be retained after a normal exit from the FOR/NEXT loop.

3.5 SOME COMMON ERRORS

(A) A branch to a wrong statement number is a logic error in a GOTO statement.

(B) A branch to a nonexistent statement number yields a common syntax error as a result of a GOTO statement.

(C) A "no-decision" decision statement, such as follows:

```
100 IF A = 0 THEN 120
120 . . .
```

causes the program to continue at line number 120 regardless of the results (true or false) of the condition between the keywords IF and THEN.

(D) A branch or transfer to a DATA statement as a result of a GOTO statement is a logic error because the DATA statement is a nonexecutable statement.

(E) Improper FOR parameters may yield an execution error, infinite loop error, or other syntax errors.

(F) Too many NEXT statements for the foot of the loop can lead to a syntax error.

(G) Incomplete FOR/NEXT pairs can lead to a double syntax error.

3.6 DEMONSTRATION PROGRAMS

```
100 REM **CALCULATE AND PRINT VALUES FOR X
105 REM    SQUARED AND X CUBED**
110 LET X = 1
115 IF X > 5 THEN 200
120 PRINT X, X^2, X^3
125 LET X = X + 1
130 GOTO 115
200 END
```

Lines 100-110 describe the program and assign a value to X. Line 115 checks to see whether the value of X is larger than 5; if so, the program ends at line 200. If not, line 120 prints values of X, X^2 and X^3. Lines 125 and 130 increment the value of X by 1 and return control to line 115.

```
100 REM **CALCULATE AND PRINT VALUES FOR X
102 REM    SQUARED AND X CUBED**
105 PRINT
110 INPUT "ENTER PASSWORD TO BEGIN THE PROGRAM"; P$
115 IF P$ = "PASSWORD" OR P$ = "P" THEN 130
120 HOME
125 GOTO 105
130 PRINT
135 FOR X = 1 TO 10 STEP 2
```

```
140 PRINT X, X^2, X^3
145 NEXT X
200 END
```

Lines 100-110 describe the program, skip a single line, and print a prompt followed by a request for a string input. Line 115 checks to see if the entered string is an appropriate match. If so, the control goes to line 130, otherwise it goes to line 120, which clears the screen. Line 125 sends the control back to line 105. Line 130 skips a single line. Lines 135-145 are a FOR/NEXT loop with an increment step of 2 for printing the values of X, X^2, and X^3. Line 200 is the end of the program.

```
100 REM **EXAMPLE USING IF/THEN/ELSE**
110 CLS
120 INPUT R$
130 IF R$="Y" THEN 140 ELSE 200
140 LET R2 = R2 + 1
150 PRINT "PROGRAMMED IN BASIC"
170 GOTO 400
200 LET R1 = R1 + 1
210 PRINT "PROGRAMMED IN PASCAL"
250 PRINT
300 GOTO 120
400 END
```

Lines 100 and 110 describe the program and clear the screen. Line 120 requests the input of a string. Line 130 either passes control to line 140 or to line 200. Lines 140-170 increment R2 by one, print a heading, and pass the control to line 400, which is the end of the program. Lines 200-300 increment R1 by one, print a heading, skip a single line, and pass the control to line 120.

CHAPTER 4

ADDITIONAL CONTROL CONCEPTS AND STATEMENTS

4.1 NESTED FOR/NEXT LOOPS

Program loops in BASIC may be contained within one another. These are called nested FOR/NEXT loops. Any number of FOR/NEXT loops may be nested, as long as they are completely contained in another loop and do not overlap. The general structure and examples of nested FOR/NEXT loops are given in Table 4.1.1.

TABLE 4.1.1   NESTED FOR/NEXT LOOPS

General Structure:		
	line no.	FOR k=initial value TO limit value
	line no.	FOR m= initial value TO limit value
		.... (other FOR statements)
	line no.	FOR j=initial value TO limit value
		... (body of loops)
	line no.	NEXT j
		.... (next to last index variable)
		.... (other index variables in reverse order)

line no.   NEXT m
line no. NEXT k

(**Note:** Use similar format with STEP aspect of the FOR/NEXT statement.)

Examples:

# 1	# 2
10 FOR A = 1 TO 10	10 FOR K = 1 TO 10 STEP 2
15 FOR B = 1 TO 10	20 FOR M = 1 TO 5 STEP 3
30 PRINT B, A	30 PRINT K, M
40 NEXT B	40 NEXT M
50 NEXT A	50 NEXT K

Notice that when nested loops are used, as shown in examples 1 and 2, each unique loop is indented for clarity.

In example #1 in Table 4.1.1, notice that when the looping is executed, in the outer loop A is initialized to one, and then the inner loop B runs until the terminal value is reached. When the terminal value of the inner loop is completed, then loop A is incremented by one again (A = 2), and the inner loop runs until the terminal value is reached. The cycling between loops A and B is repeated until the outer loop A reaches its terminal value.

Nested FOR Rule 1: If the range of a FOR statement (loop) includes another FOR statement (loop), all statements in the range of the inner FOR statement (loop) must also be within the range of the outer FOR statement (loop).

Nested FOR Rule 2: When one FOR statement (loop) is within another, the name of the control variable (index variable) for each FOR statement (loop) must be different.

Nested FOR/NEXT Rule 3: Loops in nested FOR/NEXT statements do not overlap.

4.2 ON/GOTO STATEMENT

The ON/GOTO statement is defined as a conditional GOTO statement. Depending on the current value of the numeric expression (a condition) associated with this statement, control can be transferred to multiple line numbers in a program.

The condition in the ON/GOTO statement may be a numeric variable or a numeric expression. The condition is placed between the keywords ON and GOTO. The general structure and examples of this statement are given in Table 4.2.1.

TABLE 4.2.1   THE ON/GOTO STATEMENT

General
Structure: line no. ON numeric expression GOTO line no,
                         line no, ..., line no.

Examples:

Ex. 1:   10 ON X GOTO 100, 500, 800
Ex. 2:   20 ON X/10 − 9 GOTO 900, 1100, 1300, 2000
Ex. 3:   75 ON Y GOTO 100, 800, 500, 200, 3000

The ON/GOTO statement may be utilized to implement an extension of the IF/THEN/ELSE structure discussed in Chapter 3. In particular, the ON/GOTO statement may be utilized to determine the execution of many alternatives based on an integer test. The logic flow of the ON/GOTO statement with an extension of the IF/THEN/ELSE structure, referred to as the Case structure, is shown in Figure 4.2.1.

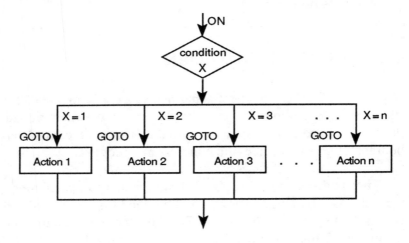

FIGURE 4.2.1—Case Structure for ON/GOTO Statement.

ON/GOTO Rule 1: When the ON/GOTO statement is executed, the integer obtained as the value of the numeric expression must never be negative, zero, or greater than the total number of line numbers in the list of statements.

ON/GOTO Rule 2: If the value of the numeric expression (condition) between the keywords ON and GOTO is 1, then the control in the program is transferred to the first line number in the list given after the keyword GOTO; if the value is 2, then the second, and so on.

ON/GOTO Rule 3: The list of statement numbers after the
keyword GOTO need not be in sequential order.

4.3 STOP STATEMENT

The STOP statement is used to terminate the program at any
point. The general structure and examples of this statement are
given in Table 4.3.1 below.

TABLE 4.3.1 THE STOP STATEMENT

General Structure:	line no. STOP
Ex. 1:	1000 STOP
Ex. 2:	9000 IF X = 5 THEN STOP

The STOP statement usually causes the following or an
equivalent message to be displayed:

BREAK IN line no.

where the line number refers to the number in the STOP statement.

4.4 SOME COMMON ERRORS

(A) Improper nesting can be caused by using the same
index within nested loops.

(B) Make sure the value of the code variable in the ON/

GOTO is always within the range given by the number of line numbers indicated within the ON/GOTO statement.

(C)   A missing GOTO statement within a logical branch leads to an error.

(D)   A common cause of infinite loops is the use of the relational operator equal (=) in the IF/THEN test.

4.5   DEMONSTRATION PROGRAMS

```
100 REM ** THREE MULTIPLICATION TABLES **
105 FOR X = 1 TO 12
110     FOR Y = 1 TO 3
120         PRINT X;" * ";Y;" = "; X*Y
130     NEXT Y
140 PRINT
150 NEXT X
160 END
```

Line 100 describes the program. Lines 105-150 are two nested FOR/NEXT loops for printing three multiplication tables with appropriate spacing. Line 140 is the end of the program.

```
100 REM **EVALUATION OF AN EXPRESSION**
110 PRINT " 8 + 2^3 * (6 - 1) = ? "
120 PRINT
125 PRINT "IS THE RESULT 48?"
130 PRINT
140 PRINT"TYPE 1 FOR YES, 2 FOR NO, 3 FOR MAYBE"
145 INPUT X
150 ON X GOTO 170, 200, 160
```

```
160 PRINT "YOU NEED TO SEE YOUR TEACHER"
165 STOP
170 PRINT "CORRECT!!"
180 GOTO 500
200 PRINT "REVIEW YOUR NOTES ON ORDER OF"
205 PRINT "OPERATIONS AND TRY AGAIN."
210 GOTO 110
500 END
```

Lines 100-140 describe the program and print strings of information separated by single lines. Line 140 requests the input of a value for X. Line 150 passes control to line 170 if X is 1, to line 200 if X is 2, and to line 160 if X is 3. Lines 160 and 165 print a message and stop the program. Lines 170 and 180 print a message and pass control to line 500, the end of the program. Lines 200-210 print a message and pass the control to line 110.

CHAPTER 5

ONE-DIMENSIONAL ARRAYS

5.1 ONE-DIMENSIONAL ARRAY CONCEPT AND SUBSCRIPTS

In BASIC, an array is a variable which is allocated a specific number of consecutive storage locations in memory, each of which can be assigned a unique value. Each value in an array is called an array element. The use of an array allows a programmer to (1) permit access to any data item that has been previously stored and (2) provide powerful capabilities to name and manipulate a large number of storage locations with data.

The variable name assigned to represent an array is called the array name. The elements in the array are distinguished from one another by subscripts, written in parentheses immediately after the array name. When each array element is referenced by only one subscript, the array is called a one-dimensional array, a vector, a list, or a one-dimensional matrix. Thus, in general, any one-dimensional array of data is given by

DN (<subscript>)

where DN denotes any allowable data name (numeric or string) and <subscript> is a numeric expression whose value is nonne-gative.

In most versions of BASIC, a one-dimensional array which is used to store numeric values is named by a single alphabetic character with the subscript in parentheses as follows:

$$X(2); \quad Y(J); \quad Z(M),$$

where X, Y, and Z represent array data names, respectively.

The DN (<subscript>) structure can be visualized as the name of a collection of adjacent memory locations (or pigeon holes) and the subscript as a pointer that allows the user to select one of the items in the collection. For example, the subscripts 1, 2, 3, 4, and 5 for an array data name X are written as

$$X(1), X(2), X(3), X(4), X(5)$$

and illustrated in the figure below.

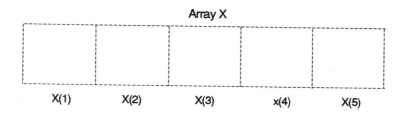

Array X

   X(1)   X(2)   X(3)   x(4)   X(5)

FIGURE 5.1.1—One-dimensional Array X(j), j=1, 2, ..., 5.

In Figure 5.1.1 there are five spaces in array X. These spaces represent locations in the computer's memory for storing data items. Only numeric data may be filled in this array as shown in Figure 5.1.2.

Array X

−2	3.7	25	0.458	−7.9
X(1)	X(2)	X(3)	X(4)	X(5)

FIGURE 5.1.2—Example of Storage of Data in Array X.

On the other hand, an alphanumeric or string array which is used to store string characters is named by a single alphabetic character followed by a dollar symbol, with the subscript in parentheses. The following are examples of alphanumeric arrays:

$$X\$(2); \quad Y\$(X); \quad Z\$(M),$$

where X\$, Y\$, and Z\$ represent appropriate array data names. Figure 5.1.3 shows an example of storage of string data in array X\$ with three subscripts.

X\$ Array

ESSENTIALS OF	BASIC	1988
X\$(1)	X\$(2)	X\$(3)

FIGURE 5.1.3—Example of Storage of Data in Array X\$.

> **Subscripted Variable Rule 1:** Subscripts must be unsigned integer constants, variables that store positive integer values, or expressions having positive integer values.

51

Subscripted Variable Rule 2: A single variable name can be used as a subscript to reference corresponding elements in different arrays.

Subscripted Variable Rule 3: Subscripts are not part of the array name.

5.2   DIM STATEMENT

The computer needs advance warning regarding the number of storage positions to reserve in its memory if subscripted variables are to be used in a program. The main function of the DIMension statement is to declare to the computer system the necessary information regarding the allocation of storage locations for arrays used in a program. The general structure of the DIM statement and some examples are given in Table 5.2.1.

TABLE 5.2.1   THE DIM STATEMENT FOR ONE-DIMENSIONAL ARRAYS

General
Structure: line no.   DIM DN(<numeric constant or data name or numeric expression>)
line no   DIM DN$(<numeric constant or data name or numeric expression>)

(where DN denotes an array name)

Examples:

Ex. 1:   50 DIM A(10)
Ex. 2:   65 DIM X(5), B$(25), K(N)
Ex. 3:   90 DIM R$(J), F$(20), B$(25), G(2)

> **DIM Rule 1:** The DIM statement is a nonexecutable statement.

> **DIM Rule 2:** The DIM statement may be placed anywhere before the first use of an array in a program.

5.3 READ, INPUT AND OUTPUT OF ONE-DIMENSIONAL ARRAYS

In a one-dimensional array data items are ordered into one column only, or into a list. Data items can be entered (read or input) into an array by use of the READ/DATA, INPUT and FOR/NEXT statements. Examples of programs using these statements are given in Table 5.3.1.

**TABLE 5.3.1   EXAMPLES OF READ/INPUT OF
ONE-DIMENSIONAL ARRAYS**

Examples:

#1	#2
(Read 5 numbers into array Y)	(Input 5 numbers into array X)
100 DIM Y(5)	100 DIM X(5)
120 FOR I=1 TO 5	120 FOR J=1 TO 5
130 READ Y(I)	130 INPUT X(J)
140 NEXT I	140 NEXT J
150 DATA 3, 5, 8,10,12	150 END
170 END	

In example #1 in Table 5.3.1, array Y accepts five values as a result of the READ/DATA statements. In example #2, array X accepts five values from the computer's keyboard as a result of the INPUT statement. The DIM statement in each example allocates sufficient storage space for each array structure.

To verify that data items are stored in an array, print out the stored data. This can be accomplished by either (1) printing out each data item immediately after it is stored or (2) printing out all the data items after all values have been stored into the array.

The elements of a data array can be manipulated by addition/ subtraction, multiplication, comparison, sorting, etc. in the same manner as any other stored values. However, subscripted data in an array can be manipulated easier than non-subscripted data since each element is identified by a pointer or unique subscript name.

Subscripted data items are useful and required in searching for an unknown value or sorting data in numerical or alphabetical order. With regards to programming routines for sorting, two popular methods (bubble sort and shell sort) are usually used. One or both of these routines are available in most BASIC programming texts.

5.4   SOME COMMON ERRORS

(A)   Failure to declare the array in a program by using the DIM statement.

(B)   Execution error resulting from the subscript range being greater than the range in the DIM statement.

(C)   Failure to zero out or initialize an array before reading of inputting data into an array.

(D)   Failure to use a loop to enter or output an array.

5.5   DEMONSTRATION PROGRAMS

```
100 HOME
105 DIM Y(5)
120 FOR I=1 TO 5
130     READ Y(I)
140     PRINT Y(I)
150 NEXT I
160 DATA 3, 1, 7, 8, 10
175 END
```

Lines 100 and 105 clear the screen and reserve five spaces in memory for the array Y. Lines 120-150 represent a FOR/NEXT loop that reads data from line 160, stores it in array Y, and prints it. Line 160 is not executed and line 175 is the end of the program.

```
100 CLS
105 DIM X(5)
120 FOR J=1 TO 5
130     READ X(J)
140 NEXT J
150 REM == PRINT ARRAY ==
160 FOR K=1 TO 5
170     PRINT X(K)
180 NEXT K
190 DATA 3, 1, 7, 8, 10
200 END
```

Lines 100 and 105 clear the screen and reserve five spaces in memory for array X. Lines 120-140 represent a FOR/NEXT loop which reads data from line 190 and stores it in array X. Lines 160-180 represent a FOR/NEXT loop which prints data from array X. Line 200 is the end of the program.

CHAPTER 6

TWO-DIMENSIONAL ARRAYS

6.1 TWO-DIMENSIONAL ARRAY CONCEPT AND SUBSCRIPTS

Two-dimensional arrays store data by rows and columns. An element within a two-dimensional array is referenced by specifying two subscripts — a row number and a column number. Thus, a two-dimensional numeric array is given and subscripted as:

array name(row, column).

A two-dimensional string array is given as:

array name$(row, column).

Storage of data items in two-dimensional arrays may be best conceptualized as a table involving rows and columns.

Figure 6.1.1 shows a 2 x 3 array (read "2 by 3 array"), which is a two-dimensional array in table format. A conceptual view of the storage locations reserved for this 2 x 3 two-dimensional array called X, with the name of each storage location specified, is also shown in Figure 6.1.1. Figure 6.1.2 shows the same array X with elements assigned to each location.

		Columns		
		1	2	3
Rows	1	X(1,1)	X(1,2)	X(1,3)
	2	X(2,1)	X(2,2)	X(2,3)

FIGURE 6.1.1—Conceptual View of Storage of 2 x 3 Array X.

		Columns		
		1	2	3
Rows	1	− 3	2.5	235
	2	10	1.34	− 59

FIGURE 6.1.2—Elements Specified in a 2 x 3 Array X.

6.2 DIM STATEMENT

A two-dimensional array must be dimensioned, just as with a one-dimensional array, in order to reserve memory locations for the array. However, some computers do not require dimension statements for two-dimensional arrays that are less than 10 x 10. On the other hand, it is good programming form to always dimension arrays regardless of their size to promote readable, transportable programs. For a two-dimensional array the DIM statement establishes the number of rows and columns that will be reserved for the array name.

Algebraic expressions may be placed in either or both subscript positions of a two-dimensional array, provided the expressions are defined before the subscript is called by the program and provided the subscripts are legal numeric values.

The general structure and some examples of the DIM statement for two-dimensional arrays are given in Table 6.2.1.

TABLE 6.2.1   THE DIM STATEMENT FOR TWO-DIMENSIONAL ARRAYS

General
Structure: line no.   DIM array name(row, column),   ...,
                          array name(row, column)

Examples:

Ex. 1:   100 DIM X(5,10)
Ex. 2:   200 DIM A$(10,15), Y(I, J), G(20, 15)

> **DIM Rule 3:** Both one and two-dimensional arrays can be dimensioned in a single DIM statement by using commas to separate each array in the list. For example:
>
> 10 DIM A(5), C(2,3), F(5)

6.3   READ, INPUT AND OUTPUT OF TWO-DIMENSIONAL ARRAYS

Data are entered (via read or input) in the same way as for one-dimensional arrays, except that both rows and columns must be considered. A nest of two FOR/NEXT loops using either the INPUT or READ/DATA statements can be used to enter data items into a two-dimensional array. For example, in the statements below the values for the rows and columns are entered by the read statement and controlled by the FOR/NEXT loops.

TABLE 6.3.1   EXAMPLE OF TWO-DIMENSIONAL FOR/NEXT LOOP

BASIC Statements for Two-Dimensional Loop	Specific Storage Locations With Their Numeric Values	
10 DIM A(3,2)		
20 FOR ROW = 1 TO 3	$A(1,1) = 2$	$A(1,2) = 3$
30 FOR COL = 1 TO 2		
40 READ A(ROW, COL)	$A(2,1) = 4$	$A(2,2) = 5$
45 PRINT A(ROW, COL)		
50 NEXT COL	$A(3,1) = 6$	$A(3,2) = 7$
60 NEXT ROW		
70 DATA 2, 3, 4, 5, 6, 7		
80 END		

The outer loop (FOR ROW / NEXT ROW) controls the three rows, and the inner loop (FOR COL / NEXT COL) controls the two columns in each row.

Output of two-dimensional arrays can be achieved in a way similar to output for one-dimensional arrays. The only exception involves printing both rows and columns. A nest of two FOR/NEXT loops with the PRINT statement is required to print the values in a two-dimensional array.

Many computers allow three-dimensional numeric and string arrays. These arrays are referenced by three subscripts. Consult your computer's manual to determine whether such three-dimensional arrays are allowed. If a three-dimensional array is allowed, then a triple nest of loops is required to load (read or input) and print the values in the array.

6.4   SOME COMMON ERRORS

Common errors associated with two-dimensional arrays usually occur as errors associated with one-dimensional arrays. See Chapter 5, Section 5.5 for a list of some common errors.

6.5   DEMONSTRATION PROGRAMS

(Read numbers into a two-dimensional array).

```
100 CLS
105 REM == PROGRAM TO READ NUMBERS INTO A ==
107 REM ==   TWO-DIMENSIONAL ARRAY        ==
110 DIM A(3,3)
120 FOR ROW=1 TO 3
130    FOR COL=1 TO 3
140        READ A(ROW,COL)
150    NEXT COL
160 NEXT ROW
170 DATA 2, 3, 4, 5, 1, 9, 8, 0, 6
200 END
```

Lines 100-110 clear the screen, describe the program, and reserve a 3 by 3 space in memory labeled array A. Lines 120-160 are two nested FOR/NEXT loops that read nine values from DATA line 170 and stores them in array A. Line 200 is the end of the program.

(Input numbers into a two-dimensional array from the keyboard).

```
100 HOME
102 REM // PROGRAM TO INPUT PAIRS OF NUMBERS //
104 REM // INTO AN ARRAY FROM THE KEYBOARD   //
105 DIM B(3,3)
120 FOR ROW=1 TO 3
130    FOR COL=1 TO 3
140       INPUT B(ROW,COL)
150    NEXT COL
160 NEXT ROW
200 END
```

Lines 100-105 clear the screen, describe the program, and reserve a 3 by 3 space in memory labeled array B. Lines 105-160 are two nested FOR/NEXT loops that allow for nine values to be inputted and stored in array B. Line 200 is the end of the program.

CHAPTER 7

FUNCTIONS AND SUBROUTINES

7.1 BASIC-SUPPLIED FUNCTIONS

The minimal BASIC language has a set of built-in operations or subprograms called BASIC-supplied or library functions. These library functions are usually mathematical operations which are predefined in the BASIC language and stored in the computer's memory by the manufacturer. They are called into action by a "calling program" or main program. The general structure of the library function or BASIC-supplied function is as follows:

function name (argument)

The function name refers to any one given in Table 7.1.1. The argument is usually the quantity to be evaluated by the function. It may be a constant, a variable, an arithmetic expression, or another function and is always enclosed in parentheses. Table 7.1.1 lists the 11 minimal BASIC-supplied functions with an example of each in a BASIC programming statement.

TABLE 7.1.1   BASIC-SUPPLIED (LIBRARY) FUNCTIONS

Function Category	Function Name	Argument Type	BASIC Example(s)
Algebraic	(Exponential, logarithmic and square root)		
	EXP(X)	Numeric value	10 Y = EXP(2*X)
	LOG(X)	+ numeric value	10 E = LOG(25)
	SQR(X)	+ numeric value	20 R = SQR(A^2)
Arithmetic	(Absolute value, greatest integer, and sign)		
	ABS(X)	Numeric value	10 Y = ABS(−4*E)
	INT(X)	Numeric value	10 Q = INT(N/D)
	SGN(X)	Numeric value	20 S = SGN(X)
Utility	(Random number generator)		
	RND or RND(X)	Depends on system	10 Y = RND or 10 Y = RND (X)
	RANDOMIZE (IBM PC only)		10 RANDOMIZE
Trigonometric	(Arctangent, cosine, sine and tangent)		
	ATN(X)	Value in radians	10 Y = ATN(X)
	COS(X)	Value in radians	10 Y = COS(2*R)
	SIN(X)	Value in radians	10 Y = 2*SIN(X+H)
	TAN(X)	Value in radians	20 Y = TAN(0.5*X)

A brief meaning of each of the aforementioned functions is given in Table 7.1.2 below.

TABLE 7.1.2 MEANINGS OF THE BASIC-SUPPLIED FUNCTIONS

Function Name /Statement	Meaning
Algebraic	
E = EXP(X)	The value of e^x is assigned to E.
L = LOG(X)	The natural log of X is assigned to L.
S = SQR(X)	The square root of X is assigned to S.
Arithmetic	
A = ABS(X)	The absolute value of X is assigned to A.
I = INT(X)	The integer part of X is assigned to I by the following rule: (a) If X is 0 or positive, then the decimal part of X is truncated and the integer part of X is assigned to I or (b) if X is negative, then the nearest integer less than or equal to the value of X is assigned to I.
S = SGN(X)	The value of X is assigned to S as follows: −1 is assigned to S when X is negative; 0 is assigned to S when X is zero; and 1 is assigned to S when X is positive.
Utility	
R = RND(1) or R=RND	A random decimal number between 0 and 1, exclusive, will be assigned to R.
RANDOMIZE	This statement is used in connection with the RND function to generate different random numbers each time the program is run.

Trigonometric

Y = ATN(X)   The arctangent of X is assigned to Y, where
                 X must be in radians.

Y = COS(X)   The cosine of X is assigned to Y, where X
                 must be in radians.

Y = SIN(X)   The sine of X is assigned to Y, where X must
                 be in radians.

Y = TAN(X)   The tangent of X is assigned to Y, where X
                 must be in radians.

7.1.1   MORE ON THE ALGEBRAIC BASIC-SUPPLIED FUNCTIONS

In the EXP function, the abbreviation EXP represents the symbol e which has a constant value of 2.71828182..., where the three dots indicate that there are other nonterminating and nonrepeating digits.

The LOG function calculates only the natural logarithm of a positive number. This function can also be used to determine the common logarithm (base 10) of a number Y by using the following BASIC statement:

10 LET X = 0.434295 * LOG(Y).

For example, log 7 = 0.845098 can be found by using the right side of the above formula 0.434295 * ln 7. The real number 0.434295, which is equal to $LOG_{10}e$, ...! is used as a constant in the statement.

The argument in the SQR function must be a positive real number to avoid an error.

7.1.2 MORE ON ARITHMETIC AND UTILITY BASIC-SUPPLIED FUNCTIONS

The INT function can be combined with the RND function to create random digits over any specified range. The following BASIC statement, used in a loop, allows for the generation of random digits over the closed interval range [A, B]:

$$10 \ X = INT((B - A + 1) * RND(1) + C) \quad \text{(for Apple)}$$

or

$$10 \ X = INT((B - A + 1) * RND + C) \quad \text{(for IBM)}$$

7.1.3 MORE ON TRIGONOMETRIC BASIC-SUPPLIED FUNCTIONS

The SIN, COS and TAN BASIC-supplied functions are used to determine the sine, cosine, and tangent of the angle X expressed in radians. To determine the cosecant, secant and cotangent of an angle X, the set of relations and BASIC statements shown in Table 7.1.3 are required.

TABLE 7.1.3   THE COSECANT, SECANT AND COTANGENT FUNCTIONS

To find	Use relation	BASIC statement
Cosecant	1/SIN(X)	10 LET Y = 1/SIN(X)
Secant	1/COS(X)	20 LET Y = 1/COS(X)
Cotangent	1/TAN(X)	30 LET Y = 1/TAN(X)

Note: "Neither" SIN(X), COS(X) nor TAN(X) can be equal to zero.

The only inverse trigonometric function supplied in minimal BASIC by the computer is the principal arctangent function ATN. This function can be used to find the principal arcsine and arccosine of X in radians as shown in Table 7.1.4. The values of the functions are only between -pi/2 and +pi/2. An example of each in BASIC is also given in the table.

TABLE 7.1.4   THE ARCSINE AND ARCCOSINE FUNCTIONS

To find	Use	BASIC statement
Arcsine	ATN(X/SQR(1–X^2))	10 LET Y = ATN(X/SQR(1–X^2))

(Note: The value of X must be between –1 and 1, not inclusive.)

Arccosine	ATN(SQR(1–X^2)/X)	20 LET Y = ATN(SQR(1–X^2)/X)

(Note: The value of X must be between – 1 and 1, inclusive, but not equal to 0.)

7.2   USER-DEFINED FUNCTIONS

User-defined functions or subprograms are those that the user defines to fit a particular programming need. These functions are not BASIC-supplied or built-in functions.

The user-defined function is defined by the DEF FN statement and can be used at any time in a program with the FN statement. The general structure and some examples of this function are given in Table 7.2.1.

The argument in the general structure of the DEF FN statement is not used as the actual argument when the function is called. Thus, the argument is referred to as a "dummy argument."

TABLE 7.2.1 THE DEF FN STATEMENT

General
Structure: line no.   DEF FN function name(argument) =
                  expression

Once the DEF FN function is specified in a program, then the following forms may be used within
the program:

line no.   expression = FN function name
             (argument)
and

line no.   INPUT/OUTPUT statement FN function
             name (argument)

(**Note:** The keyword DEF is a signal to the BASIC
translator that this line is a user-defined function.)

Examples:

Ex. 1:   10 DEF FNY(X) = SQR(A*EXP(X^2))
Ex. 2:   20 DEF FNH(X) = X + 0.5*SIN(X − 2)

– –

Ex. 3:   30 PRINT FNH(A), FNY(B)
Ex. 4:   40 V = FNH(INT(A))

Examples of some common invalid DEF FN statements and
some possible corresponding valid DEF FN statements are shown
in Table 7.2.2.

TABLE 7.2.2   INVALID AND CORRESPONDING VALID DEF FN STATEMENTS

Invalid DEF FN Statements	Valid DEF FN Statements
10 DEF(X) = 2*X (Error: Missing function name)	10 DEF FNF(X) = 2 * X
20 DEF FN1(Y) = 3*Y (Error: 1 is invalid name.)	20 DEF FNR(Y) = 3 * Y
30 DEF FNB(A$) = RIGHT$(A$,2) (Error: String dummy variable is not allowed without string function name.)	30 DEF FNB$(A$) = RIGHT$(A$,2)

DEF Rule 1: When a function is defined by a DEF statement the function may be used anywhere in the program.

DEF Rule 2: A function defined by a DEF statement is usually limited by a single statement.

DEF Rule 3: The DEF statement is a nonexecutable statement.

7.3   SUBROUTINES/THE GOTO AND RETURN STATEMENTS

A sequence of successive statements within a program that accomplishes a specific purpose within the program is referred to as a subroutine. It is used when the same group of statements is needed many times in a program. A subroutine is usually located at the end of the main program body.

Conceptually a subroutine interacts with the main program as shown in Figure 7.3.1.

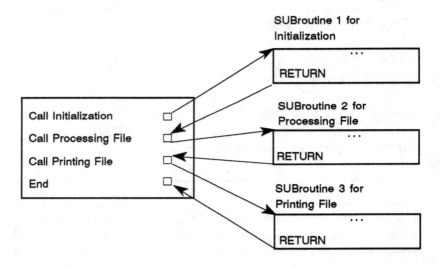

FIGURE 7.3.1—Conceptual View of Relationship Between Main Program and Subroutines.

7.3.1   THE GOSUB STATEMENT

Each subroutine is accessed or called with the use of a GOSUB statement. The general structure and example of this statement is given in Table 7.3.1.

TABLE 7.3.1   THE GOSUB STATEMENT

General Structure: line no.   GOSUB line number

Examples:

Ex. 1:   1000 GOSUB 7000
Ex. 2:   1010 GOSUB 8000: GOSUB 9000
Ex. 3:   1020 IF X > 5 THEN GOSUB 10000

When the GOSUB statement is executed in a program the main program transfers control to the location of the subroutine. The GOSUB statement is an unconditional transfer statement.

7.3.2   THE RETURN STATEMENT

The RETURN statement is placed in the program at the end of the subroutine. Execution of this statement returns control to the main program at the statement directly following the GOSUB statement. The general structure and an example of the statement are given in Table 7.3.2.

TABLE 7.3.2   THE RETURN STATEMENT

General
Structure: line no. RETURN

Example:

```
1000  INPUT N, D
1010  GOSUB 9000
1020  PRINT X
        . . .
        . . .
7000  END
9000  REM ** Begin subroutine **
9010  X = N/D
9025  RETURN
```

> **GOSUB/RETURN Rule 1:** The calling program can be the main program or another subroutine.

> **GOSUB/RETURN Rule 2:** A subroutine can be placed anywhere within the program. However, the subroutine is usually placed after the main program.

> **GOSUB/RETURN Rule 3:** An entry to a given subroutine does not have to be made at the same initial statement each time the subroutine is called.

> **GOSUB/RETURN Rule 4:** A subroutine may be terminated at more than one statement. Thus, a subroutine may be terminated prior to the RETURN statement.

7.4 ON/GOSUB STATEMENT

ON/GOSUB is a statement which transfers control in the same way as does the ON/GOTO statement. The general structure and examples are given in Table 7.4.1.

TABLE 7.4.1   ON/GOSUB STATEMENT

General
Structure: line no.   ON expression GOSUB line 1, line 2,
. . .

Examples:

Ex. 1:   100 ON/10 GOSUB 1000, 9000, 10000
Ex. 2:   150 ON Y + 2 GOSUB 8000
Ex. 3:   200 ON X GOSUB 1000, 5000, 4000, 9000, 10000

The expression after the keyword ON is evaluated to an integer and sends control to the various line numbers following the keyword GOSUB. These line numbers indicate the subroutines. If the expression is evaluated to be 1 then the control is transferred to the first line number after GOSUB; a value of 2 sends the control to the second line number after GOSUB; etc. The RETURN statement sends the control to the next statement after the ON/GOSUB statement.

7.4.1 DIFFERENCES BETWEEN GOSUB AND GOTO OR ON/GOSUB AND ON/GOTO

The main difference between a GOSUB and a GOTO statement, or between an ON/GOSUB and an ON/GOTO statement, lies in the execution of a subroutine. For a GOSUB or ON/GOSUB, the following occurs:

(1) The main program calls or transfers control to the subroutine.

(2) The subroutine that has been called executes and performs a particular or recurring task for the main program.

(3) The RETURN statement of the subroutine transfers control back to the statement immediately following the GOSUB or ON/GOSUB which referenced the subroutine.

The GOTO or ON/GOTO do not have the aforementioned features.

7.5 SOME COMMON ERRORS

(A) A zero or negative argument for some library functions or an incorrect number in arguments of user-defined functions may lead to a fatal execution error.

(B) An overflow in the execution of the EXP function leads to an error.

(C) Improper use of the RND function may lead to logic errors.

(D) An inadvertent entry into a subroutine from the main program that is not separated from the subroutine can cause the program to stop.

(E) Using the same variable in the main part of the program and in the subroutines can inadvertently change the value of the variable in the subroutines, which can cause errors.

(F) Missing function name in a DEF statement results in an error.

7.6 DEMONSTRATION PROGRAMS

```
100 REM **FIND HYPOTENUSE OF RIGHT TRIANGLES**
110 PRINT "LEGS A AND B OF RIGHT TRIANGLES"
111 PRINT "ARE GIVEN."
120 FOR I = 10 TO 15
125     FOR J = -1 TO -5 STEP -.255
130         PRINT
135         LET A = INT(ABS(J))
137         LET B = I
140         PRINT "LEG A = ";A;" AND LEG B = ";B
145         LET C = SQR(A^2 + B^2)
150         PRINT "LENGTH OF HYPOTENUSE C = ";C
```

```
155    NEXT J
160 NEXT I
200 END
```

Lines 100 and 110 describe the program and document the variables. Lines 120-160 are two nested FOR/NEXT loops. The inner loop (J) increments by -0.255 and then assigns values to legs A and B, calculates the hypotenuse and prints the heading and the values of A, B and C. The outer loop continues this process five times. Line 200 is the end of the program.

```
100 DEF FNY(X) = (2*X + 4)/4
120 LET X1 = 5
130 LET X2 = FNY(X1)
140 PRINT X2
200 END
```

Line 100 is the function described by the user and it is stored in memory until it is called up. Line 120 initializes X1 to five. Line 130 calls up the user function and substitutes the value of X1 for X and stores the value in location X2. Line 140 prints the value of X2 and line 200 is the end of the program.

```
100 REM ** MAIN PROGRAM **
110 PRINT "THIS IS AN EXAMPLE OF A SUBROUTINE."
120 GOSUB 500
130 PRINT "THIS STATEMENT IS PRINTED AFTER A DELAY"
140 GOSUB 500
145 GOSUB 500
150 PRINT "THIS STATEMENT IS PRINTED AFTER A"
151 PRINT "LONGER DELAY"
```

```
200 END
500 REM ** DELAY SUBROUTINE **
510 FOR I = 1 TO 10000
520 NEXT I
530 RETURN
```

Lines 100 and 110 describe the program and print identifying information. Lines 120-150 direct the computer to the subroutine for execution, print a message in line 130, direct the computer to the subroutine twice for execution, and print a message in line 150. Lines 500-530 describe the subroutine and include a FOR/NEXT empty loop for the delay subroutine. The end of the program, line 200, precedes the subroutine.

PART II:
ENHANCED BASIC

BASIC statements included in Part II are not in the subset of the language referred to as **minimal** BASIC by the proposed ANSI standard. Thus, variations exist from computer system to computer system relative to the structure of BASIC statements covered in Part II. Thus, this part of BASIC is referred to as **enhanced** BASIC. Structure differences in enhanced BASIC statements are only noted for Apple and IBM PCs.

Enhanced BASIC will **only** include formatted output, data files, matrix operations, and string functions. Check the programming manual for your computer system for other enhanced BASIC functions and statements, such as those involving sound and graphics.

CHAPTER 8

FORMATTED OUTPUT

8.1 MORE ON THE PRINT STATEMENT

The PRINT statement as indicated in Chapter 1 permits the outputting of multiple data values, string values, or combinations. The punctuation used in the instruction determines how the output appears across a horizontal line on the monitor screen or print page. In minimal BASIC the 40-character line was the standard. However, most extended BASIC printers and monitor screens today have the capacity to product 80 characters per horizontal line. If the extended BASIC instruction directs the output of more than 80 characters on one print page line, the computer system applies an automatic "wraparound" feature to accommodate the characters.

The maximum horizontal line character capacity on monitor screens varies from one computer system to another from a minimum width of 40 characters on some computer systems to a maximum of 80 characters on others.

Extended BASIC for the IBM PC divides the 80-character horizontal print page line into five (5) print zones, or fields. For the Apple, the standard 40-character horizontal print page line is divided into three (3) print zones. Table 8.1.1 shows the zone columns for both the IBM PC and Apple Computer.

TABLE 8.1.1   COLUMNS OF PRINT ZONES

IBM PC		Apple	
Zone	Columns	Zone	Columns
1	1 - 14	1	1 -16
2	15 - 28	2	17 - 32
3	29 - 42	3	33 - 40
4	43 - 56		
5	57 - 80		

The Apple computer has the capacity to switch from the 40-character screen to the 80-character screen by typing PR#3 and pressing the Return Key. To return to the original 40-column screen from an 80-column screen, press and release the ESC key, then hold down the CONTROL (CTRL) KEY and press Q.

8.1.1   ZONE OR FIELD SPACING

When a data name or constant, either numeric or literal, is followed by a comma in a PRINT statement, the next data name or constant is displayed or printed in the next zone. The following Table 8.1.2 shows an example of field spacing applied to both the IBM PC and Apple Computer.

TABLE 8.1.2   EXAMPLES OF FIELD SPACING IN EXTENDED BASIC

Values of Variables		BASIC Statement
$A = 8$	$B = 10$	
$C = 1$	$D = 5$	
$E = -7$		10 PRINT A, B, C, D, E

Output for IBM PC (80-column monitor screen or printer)

8	10	1	5	−7

Output for Apple (40-column monitor screen or printer)

8	10	1
5	−7	

8.1.2   THE LPRINT STATEMENT

The LPRINT statement is used in an extended BASIC program for printer output in the same fashion as the PRINT statement described in Chapter 1 is used for monitor output in minimal BASIC. However, the LPRINT statement is not available on the Apple Computer. The general format and examples of this statement are shown in Table 8.1.3.

TABLE 8.1.3   THE LPRINT STATEMENT

General
Structure: line no. LPRINT "string characters"
              and
              line no. LPRINT

Examples:
Ex. 1:   100 LPRINT "Welcome to ESSENTIALS OF BASIC"
Ex. 2:   110 LPRINT
Ex. 3:   120 LPRINT "How are you today?"

Caution: Not available on the Apple.

Recall that the LPRINT statement causes output at the printer only. Thus, lines 100 and 120 in Table 8.1.3 produce on the printer the strings inside the quotes and line 110 produces a blank line as follows:

Welcome to ESSENTIALS OF BASIC

How are you today?

The LPRINT and PRINT statements may be used in the same program to output information to both the monitor and the printer.

8.1.3 THE PR#0 AND PR#1 COMMANDS

In order to produce output at the printer on the Apple, the printer must be activated by typing the system command PR#1. Once this is done the standard PRINT statement in the BASIC program causes the output to appear on the printer. Typing the PR#0 command causes the program output to return to the monitor-only display. Consider the example:

```
100 PRINT "The ESSENTIALS OF BASIC"
110 PRINT
120 PRINT "Is this book helpful?"
```

This program produces output at the printer if the system command PR#1 is typed before the program is executed. The results appear as follows:

The ESSENTIALS OF BASIC

Is this book helpful?

The PR#1 and PR#0 commands may be used as programming statements in a program in order to permit simultaneous output at the printer and the monitor using an Apple Computer. The general structure and an example of the use of these commands in a program setting are shown in Table 8.1.4.

82

**TABLE 8.1.4   PR#1 AND PR#0 AS PROGRAMMING
                STATEMENTS**

General
Structure: line no. PR#1
                line no. PR#0

Example:

```
10 PRINT "The ESSENTIALS OF BASIC"
15 PR#1
20 PRINT "The ESSENTIALS OF BASIC"
30 PR#0
50 END
```

Caution: This is not available on the IBM PC.

The program in Table 8.1.4 produces output both to the monitor screen and the printer in the following form:

    The ESSENTIALS OF BASIC.

8.2   THE PRINT USING STATEMENT

Compared to the PRINT statement, the PRINT USING statement is far more useful in controlling the format of a program that requires the generation of certain data processing output. With the PRINT USING statement the programmer can do the following:

(1)   Specify the exact image of a line of output.

(2)   Force decimal point alignment when printing columns in tables.

(3)   Specify that commas be inserted into a number.

(4)   Control the number of digits displayed for a number.

(5)   Specify that a + or – sign be displayed with a number.

(6)   Assign a dollar sign to a number.

(7)   Force justification of a string of values.

(8)   Specify that only the first character of a string be printed.

(9)   Specify automatic rounding of a decimal number.

There are special symbols used in the structure of the PRINT USING statement to let BASIC know when to execute the various formats. A list of these symbols is given in Section 8.3, Table 8.3.1. The general structure of the PRINT USING statement and some examples are given in Table 8.2.1.

TABLE 8.2.1   THE PRINT USING STATEMENT

General
Structure: line no.   PRINT USING "format"; variable
                          expressions

Examples:

Ex. 1: 100 PRINT USING "##.#"; X
Ex. 2: 125 PRINT USING "#,###.##"; D
Ex. 3: 200 PRINT USING "Amt is: **$#,###.## of budget."; B

Caution: The PRINT USING statement is not available on the Apple.

8.3 TYPES OF OUTPUT FIELDS

The information shown in Table 8.3.1 represents symbols which appear in the format component of the structure of the PRINT USING statement. Also, these symbols represent the types of output values or fields.

TABLE 8.3.1 LIST OF FORMAT SYMBOLS FOR PRINT USING STATEMENT

Symbol	Use	Examples
#	Reserves space for 1 digit Reserves space for 3 digits	# ###
.	Location of decimal point within number sign (#) field	##.###
,	Location of one or more commas with a # field	#,###,###.##
+ or −	Displays + or − sign before or after the # field	+#### −###.#
$$	Display a single dollar prior to a # field	$$###.##
**	Replace leading blanks in a # field with asterisks	**###,###
^^^^	Output in scientific notation field	#.##^^^^
!	Outputs first character of a string field	!
\\	Output only the first two characters of a string field	\\
&	Outputs any size string field	&

8.4 SOME COMMON ERRORS

(A) If the width of the field specified is smaller than the
     value to be printed then a field overflow occurs.

(B) The use of image lines in PRINT USING for alignment
     of output may result in an error because related labeled
     output does not align visually. A paper design of output
     helps to correct this error.

8.5 DEMONSTRATION PROGRAMS

```
100 REM **PROGRAM TO GENERATE THE MULTIPLICATION TABLE**
120 CLS
130 PRINT " x ! 0   1   2   3   4   5   6   7   8   9  10  11  12"
140 PRINT "---!-----------------------------------------------"
150 FOR M = 0 TO 12
160    PRINT USING "###   !"; M;
170    FOR F = 0 TO 12
175     PRINT USING "####"; M * F;
180    NEXT F
185 NEXT M
190 PRINT
195 PRINT "-------------------------------------------------------"
200 END
```

Lines 100-140 describe the program, clear the screen and
print labels for the table. Lines 150-185 are two nested loops in
which the values of the variables are printed using preassigned
formats. Lines 190 and 195 skip a line and print the bottom line
of the table. Line 200 is the end of the program.

```
100 REM ** PROGRAM TO DEMONSTRATE DIFFERENT PRINT USING **
110 REM ** SYMBOLS **
115 CLS
120 PRINT USING "  ###"; 125
130 PRINT USING "  ###.###"; 12.4535
140 PRINT USING "  #,###.##"; 1245.35
150 A$ = "Nearly ##### persons donated ##,###,###.## this year."
160 LET G = 75750
170 PRINT USING F$; G, 12255675.00#
180 PRINT
190 PRINT USING "My donation was **$####.##."; 250.2
200 END
```

Lines 100-140 describe the program, clear the screen, and print values in preassigned formats. Line 150 assigns a string including preassigned formats. Lines 160-190 assign a value to G, print a string with preassigned formats, skip a single line and print another string with a preassigned format. Line 200 is the end of the program.

```
100 CLS
110 LET C = 10.25
115 LET D = 2.45
120 LET E = 12.2
125 LET F = 195
130 PRINT USING "##.##     #.#     ##"; C, D, E
140 PRINT
150 PRINT USING "##.##     #.#     ##"; E, F, C
160 PRINT
170 PRINT USING "##.##     #.#     ##"; D, E, F
200 END
```

Lines 100-125 clear the screen and assign values to C, D, E, and F, respectively. Lines 130-170 print the values in preassigned formats with a single line skipped between each printing. Line 200 is the end of the program.

CHAPTER 9

DATA FILES

The computer utilizes two different popular data file types: sequential and random-access. The sequential file is used in situations requiring data to be recalled in the same order as it was originally stored in the file. On the other hand, if information is to be retrieved from a random location in the file, then random-access files are better suited.

9.1 SEQUENTIAL FILES

File handling statements required to create and process a sequential file are given below. Note that D$ = CHR$(4) when using the Apple Computer.

9.1.1 OPENING A SEQUENTIAL FILE

Before a file can be accessed, it must be OPENed. This can be done by using the general structure given in Table 9.1.1.

TABLE 9.1.1 THE OPEN STATEMENT FOR A SEQUENTIAL FILE

General
Structure: (for Apple)
line no. PRINT CHR$(4); "OPEN filename"

or
line no. D$=CHR$(4)
line no. PRINT D$; "OPEN filename"

— — — — — — — — — — — — — — — — — — —

(for IBM)
line no. OPEN "mode", channel, "filename"

Examples:

(for Apple)
Ex. 1:   20 PRINT CHR$(4); "OPEN PAYROLL"
          or
          10 D$ = CHR$(4)
          20 PRINT D$; "OPEN PAYROLL"

— — — — — — — — — — — — — — — — — — —

(for IBM)
Ex. 2:   20 OPEN "O", 1, "PAYROLL. TXT"
          ("O" denotes output mode.)

When a line number for opening a file in a program is executed, the Disk Operating System (DOS) for the computer system will create a new file with the new filename. The filename must begin with a letter. Once a file has been opened, data can be written or read into the file.

9.1.2   FILE BUFFER

Data are transferred into the sequential file by means of a file buffer. The DOS usually transfers data to the disk in blocks. A file buffer is the part of the memory that is set aside as a data transfer area.

9.1.3   WRITING DATA TO A SEQUENTIAL FILE

To write to the beginning of a sequential file, the file must be OPENed. The WRITE statement is used with a PRINT CHR$(4)

statement or a control (CTRL) – D command to tell the Apple Computer that the following PRINT statements are to write to a sequential file and not to the display screen.

For the IBM PC, the WRITE # statement is used with INPUT statements to write to a sequential file. Information contained in the variables stated in the WRITE # statement will be placed or written in the file associated with the specific channel # and not displayed on the display screen. The WRITE # statement automatically places quotation marks around string data and commas between both string and numeric data in a sequential file. The commas and quotation marks act as markers so that the IBM PC can tell the difference between data items when they are to be read from the file.

The general structure and examples of the appropriate WRITE statements when writing data to a sequential data file on the Apple and IBM PC are shown in Table 9.1.2.

TABLE 9.1.2   STATEMENTS FOR WRITING DATA TO A SEQUENTIAL FILE

General
Structure: (for Apple)
      line no. PRINT CHR$(4); "WRITE filename"

— — — — — — — — — — — — — — — — — —

      (for IBM)
      line no. WRITE #<channel>, variable, ...

Examples:

(for Apple)
Ex. 1:   20 PRINT CHR$(4); "WRITE HOURS"
       25 PRINT "FILE THIS STATEMENT"

— — — — — — — — — — — — — — — — — —

(for IBM)
Ex. 2:   20 INPUT "NAME"; EMPLOYEE$, HOURS
       25 WRITE #1, EMPLOYEE$, HOURS

9.1.4 READING DATA FROM A SEQUENTIAL FILE

To read information from a sequential file, the Apple Computer requires the use of the READ and PRINT CHR$(4) statements, followed by INPUT statements for reading individual lines of data from the file. In particular, data that have been stored in a sequential data file can be accessed with a READ statement which must follow an OPEN command. The BASIC statement which actually retrieves data from the sequential file is the INPUT statement, which signifies that data is to be entered from a storage device such as a diskette or hard disk.

For the IBM PC, the INPUT # statement is used to read information from a sequential file. It is important that the order in which the variables are listed in the INPUT # statement be the same as the order of the variables in the WRITE # statement used in creating the file.

The general structure and examples of the appropriate read statements when reading data from a sequential data file on the IBM PC and Apple are shown in Table 9.1.3.

TABLE 9.1.3   STATEMENTS FOR READING DATA FROM A SEQUENTIAL FILE

General
Structure: (for Apple)
              line no. PRINT CHR$(4); "READ filename"
              line no. INPUT variable

_ _

              (for IBM)
              line no. INPUT #<channel>, variable, ...

Examples:

(for Apple)
Ex. 1:   20 PRINT CHR$(4); "READ DATA"

92

```
25 INPUT B$
30 PRINT B$
```

— — — — — — — — — — — — — — — — — — — —

(for IBM)

Ex. 2:   20 INPUT #2, EMPLOYEE$, HOURS
           25 PRINT EMPLOYEE$, HOURS

9.1.5   UPDATING A SEQUENTIAL FILE

For the Apple Computer, the APPEND command is used to add data to an existing sequential file. The APPEND command is used instead of an OPEN command in order to add to an already existing sequential file. The APPEND command will open the file and move a pointer to the end of the file named so that any data which is read to the file will be added to the end of the current file. The general structure of the APPEND command and examples are shown in Table 9.1.4

For the IBM PC, the (A)ppend mode is used in the OPEN statement to append new information to an existing sequential file. When an OPEN command is executed with the (O)utput mode, the computer opens the file and prepares to write to it. If the (O)utput mode is used to append new information to the file then the new information added will be written over that which was at the beginning of the file, thus destroying the old information. To avoid this loss of data, the "A" mode instructs the computer to write new information at the end of the sequential file. The general structure and examples of the (A)ppend mode are shown in Table 9.1.4.

TABLE 9.1.4   COMMANDS FOR UPDATING A SEQUENTIAL FILE

General
Structure: (for Apple)
               line no. PRINT CHR$(4); "APPEND filename"

— — — — — — — — — — — — — — — — — — — —

(for IBM)
line no. OPEN "A", 1, "filename"
(**Note:** The remainder of the statements should follow the procedure used for writing data to file.)

Examples:

(for Apple)
Ex. 1:   20 PRINT CHR$(4); "APPEND HOURS"
           or
           20 D$ = CHR$(4)
           30 PRINT D$; "APPEND SAMPLE"

(for IBM)
Ex. 2:   20 OPEN "A", 1, "JOB"
           25 INPUT "NAME"; EMPLOYEE$
           30 WRITE #1, EMPLOYEE$

TABLE 9.1.5   DELETING A SEQUENTIAL FILE

General
Structure: (for Apple)
          line no. PRINT CHR$(4); "OPEN file"
          line no. PRINT CHR$(4); "DELETE file"

          (for IBM)
          line no. KILL "filename"

Examples:

(for Apple)
Ex. 1:   10 PRINT CHR$(4); "OPEN HOURS"
           20 PRINT CHR$(4); "DELETE HOURS"
           30 PRINT CHR$(4); "OPEN HOURS"
           40 PRINT CHR$(4); "WRITE HOURS"
           50 PRINT "RECORD 0"
           60 PRINT CHR$(4); "CLOSE HOURS"

```
(for IBM)
Ex. 2:    10  OPEN "I", 1, "B:SAMPLE.TXT"
          20  . . .

               . . .

          90  KILL "B:SAMPLE.TXT"
```

To delete or completely erase an Apple sequential file, the DELETE command is used with an opened file. For the IBM PC, the KILL statement may be used to completely erase a sequential file. The general structure of the DELETE command and KILL statement and examples are shown in Table 9.1.5.

9.1.6 CLOSING A SEQUENTIAL FILE

Any sequential file that has been previously opened must be closed. The CLOSE statement is used to communicate the closing procedure. By closing the file, you ensure that all data will be written out of the file buffer and the closed sequential file will be put on the disk's catalog or list of files. The general structure and examples of the CLOSE statement for the Apple and IBM are shown in Table 9.1.6.

TABLE 9.1.6 CLOSING A SEQUENTIAL FILE

General
Structure: (for Apple)
               line no. PRINT CHR$(4); "CLOSE filename"
               _ _ _ _ _ _ _ _ _ _ _ _ _ _ _ _ _ _
               (for IBM)
               line no. CLOSE <channel>

Examples:

```
(for Apple)
Ex. 1:    50  PRINT CHR$(4); "CLOSE HOURS"
Ex. 2:    50  D$ = CHR$(4)
          60  PRINT D$; "CLOSE SAMPLE"
```

Ex. 3:   50 CLOSE 1
Ex. 4:   50 CLOSE 2
Ex. 5:   50 CLOSE 1, 2

The following rules summarize the OPEN, WRITE, READ, and CLOSE statements for a sequential file.

OPEN Rule 1: A file must be opened before it can be read from or written to.

OPEN Rule 2: If a file is opened for input, it must already exist on auxiliary storage.

OPEN Rule 3: If a file is opened for output and it exists on auxiliary storage, it is deleted before it is opened.

OPEN Rule 4: A filenumber cannot be assigned to more than one file at a time.

WRITE Rule 1 (Apple only): The PRINT statements following WRITE command for sequential files are not treated in the same manner as PRINT statements are in other parts of a program.

WRITE Rule 2 (IBM only): The WRITE # command for sequential files requires a channel number, usually denoted by an integer from 1 to 15.

> **READ Rule 1 (Apple only):** When a READ statement is executed for a sequential file the data in the file will be read until it is empty or until a different DOS command is executed.

> **READ Rule 2 (IBM only):** The INPUT # statement for sequential files requires a channel number, usually denoted by an integer from 1 to 15.

> **CLOSE Rule 1:** A file must be opened before it can be closed.

9.1.7 PROTECTING A FILE

A sequential or any other file on a diskette or hard disk can be protected from accidental erasing by use of the lock or protect command for the particular computer system. Once a file is locked or protected, it cannot be deleted, changed or renamed until it is unlocked or unprotected.

9.2 RANDOM-ACCESS FILES

File handling statements required to create and process a random-access file are given in the sub-sections below. In each subsection, note that for the Apple Computer D$ = CHR$(4).

9.2.1 OPENING A RANDOM-ACCESS FILE

The general structure and examples of the OPEN statement for creating or opening a random-access file for the Apple and IBM computers are shown in Table 9.2.1.

TABLE 9.2.1 OPENING A RANDOM-ACCESS FILE

General
Structure: (for Apple)
            line no.   PRINT D$; "OPEN filename, L record
                       length n"

— — — — — — — — — — — — — — — —

           (for IBM)
           line no.   OPEN "R", <channel>, "filename",
                       record length n

Examples:

(for Apple)
Ex. 1:   20 PRINT D$; "OPEN WAGES, L 15"
Ex. 2:   20 PRINT D$; "OPEN BOOKS, L 30"

— — — — — — — — — — — — — — — —

(for IBM)
Ex. 3:   20 OPEN "R",3, "PRESIDENTS", 40

For a random-access file on the Apple Computer, the comma
following the filename separates the length parameter, which is
preceded by the letter L. To determine the length to be used in
the OPEN statement, 1 must be added to the number of characters in the longest record in the data. The extra byte is required to
store the carriage return indicating the end of the record. For the
IBM PC, the "R" and the integer after the comma denote a
random-access file on a channel represented by the integer. The
final number n in the OPEN statement represents the length of
each record in the file.

9.2.2 WRITING DATA TO A RANDOM-ACCESS FILE

The general structure and examples of the statements used
with Apple and IBM computers to write data into a random-
access file are shown in Table 9.2.2. For the Apple, the WRITE

statement is used with the PRINT D\$ (where D\$ = CHR\$(4)) in order to write data into the file. For the IBM, the FIELD statement, LSET and/or RSET command(s), and PUT statement are used. The FIELD statement partitions the buffer into regions where each holds a string and is referenced by a specific string variable. The LSET and RSET commands transfer the strings in the field to the buffer. The PUT statement actually transfers the data in the buffer to a record in the file.

TABLE 9.2.2   WRITING DATA TO RANDOM-ACCESS FILE

General Structure:	(for Apple) line no. PRINT D\$; "WRITE filename, R"; record no.
	(for IBM) line no. FIELD \<channel\>, \<length\> AS \<string variable\>
	line no. LSET \<string var from FIELD\> = \<string to be transferred to buffer\> and/or RSET \<string var from FIELD\> = \<string to be transferred to buffer\>
	line no. PUT \<channel\>, \<record number\>

Examples:

(for Apple)
Ex. 1:   20 PRINT D\$; "WRITE MBOOK,R"; 15
Ex. 2:   20 PRINT CHR\$(4);"WRITE MBOOK, R"; 15

(for IBM)
Ex. 3:   20 FIELD 1, 10 AS BK\$
Ex. 4:   25 LSET BK\$ = "TEN WORDS**"
Ex. 5:   30 PUT 1

9.2.3   READING DATA FROM A RANDOM-ACCESS FILE

To read data from a random-access file requires the use of the PRINT CHR$(4) with the READ statement for the Apple and the GET and FIELD statements for the IBM. The GET statement performs the opposite function of the PUT statement. It is used to transfer information in a record on the disk to the buffer associated with the file. A FIELD statement must be used in order to partition the buffer for the data that is to be transferred into it. The general structure and examples of these statements are shown below in Table 9.2.3.

TABLE 9.2.3   READING DATA FROM RANDOM-ACCESS FILE

General
Structure: (for Apple)
              line no.   PRINT D$; "READ filename, R";
                         record no.

 — — — — — — — — — — — — — — — — — —

              (for IBM)
              line no.   GET <channel>, <record number>

Examples:

(for Apple)
Ex. 1:   20 PRINT D$; "READ BOOKS,R"; 4
Ex. 2:   20 PRINT CHR$(4);"READ BOOKS, R"; 4

 — — — — — — — — — — — — — — — — — —

(for IBM)
Ex. 3:   20 GET 2, 4
Ex. 4:   20 GET 2, RECORD

9.2.4   CLOSING A RANDOM-ACCESS DATA FILE

The general structure and examples for the CLOSE statement of the random-access file are the same as those given in Table 9.1.5.

9.2.5   THE LOC FUNCTION

The LOC function is available in extended BASIC for the IBM PC. It is useful when working with random-access files. The function returns the record number used in the last GET or PUT executed on a given channel. The BASIC statement

$$10 \ A = LOC(2)$$

will assign to the variable A the record number used in the last PUT or GET operation performed on channel 2. The LOC function will return 0 until a PUT or GET is executed.

9.3   SOME COMMON ERRORS

(A)   Failure to use the appropriate system command or statement to reserve storage space for the file leads to an error.

(B)   An error is created by failing to properly open and close the file.

(C)   Absence of any random-access file parameter creates an error.

9.4   DEMONSTRATION PROGRAMS

```
100 REM ** OPENING AND WRITING DATA TO A RANDOM **
102 REM ** DATA FILE ON AN APPLE COMPUTER **
105 HOME
110 LET D$ = CHR$(4)
115 PRINT D$;"OPEN BOOKS, L 20"
120 INPUT "ENTER RECORD #"; I
125 INPUT "AUTHOR NAME ";A$
```

```
130 INPUT "BOOK NAME ";B$
135 PRINT D$;"WRITE BOOKS,R";I
140 PRINT A$
145 PRINT B$
150 PRINT D$
155 INPUT "ANOTHER RECORD? (Y OR N)"; X$
160 IF X$ = "Y" THEN 120
165 PRINT D$;"CLOSE BOOKS"
200 END
```

Lines 100-105 describe the Apple program and clear the screen. Line 110 initializes the disk command CHR$(4). Line 115 opens the random data file BOOKS in which each record must be 20 characters long. Lines 120-130 ask for information to be entered into the record. Line 135 tells the computer that the entered record will be written to the file. Lines 140-150 write the record to the file. Line 155 asks if another record is to be added and 160 sends the control to line 120 if the answer is yes, otherwise line 165 closes the file and line 200 ends the program.

```
100 REM ** OPENING A SEQUENTIAL DATA FILE **
105 REM ** ON AN IBM PC **
108 CLS
110 OPEN "O", 1, "B:BOOK. FILE"
120 FOR N = 1 TO 5
130    INPUT "BOOK NAME"; BKNAME$
140    INPUT "AUTHOR NAME"; ARNAME$
150    INPUT "NUMBER BK"; NUMBER
160    WRITE #1, BKNAME$, ARNAME$, NUMBER
170    PRINT
180 NEXT N
190 CLOSE 1
200 END
```

Lines 100-108 describe the IBM program and clear the screen. Line 110 opens the sequential file B:BOOK. FILE on channel 1. Lines 120-180 represent a FOR/NEXT loop in which data are inputted from the keyboard for each record and the WRITE # command actually writes the data to the file. Line 190 closes the file that was previously opened on channel 1.

```
100 REM ** READING A SEQUENTIAL FILE NAMED DATA **
105 REM ** WHICH ALREADY EXISTS ON DISK **
110 REM ** ON AN APPLE COMPUTER **
120 HOME
130 LET D$ = CHR$(4)
140 PRINT D$; "OPEN DATA"
150 PRINT D$; "READ DATA"
160 INPUT A$
170 PRINT A$
180 PRINT D$, "CLOSE DATA"
200 END
```

Lines 100-120 describe the Apple program and clear the screen. Line 130 initializes the disk CHR$(4) command. Line 140 opens the sequential file DATA. Lines 150-170 read the data from the file and then print it. Line 180 closes the file. Line 200 ends the program.

```
100 REM   N$ = Name, PR$, ADDR$, A$ = Address
105 REM   PROGRAM TO CREATE RANDOM-ACCESS FILE
107 REM   ADDR.TXT AND ALLOW 5 NAMES AND ADDRESSES
110 REM   TO BE PLACED ON FILE ON AN IBM PC
115 CLS
120 OPEN "R", 1, "B:ADDR.TXT", 45
130 FIELD 1, 15 AS PR$, 30 AS ADDR$
```

```
140 FOR L = 1 TO 5
150     INPUT "NAME"; N$
155     INPUT "ADDRESS"; A$
160     LSET PR$ = N$
170     LSET ADDR$ = A$
180     PUT 1
190     PRINT
200 NEXT L
250 CLOSE 1
500 END
```

Lines 100-115 describe the IBM program and clear the screen. Line 120 opens the random-access file B:ADDR.TXT on channel 1 with each record containing 45 characters. Line 130 organizes the buffer so that data can be sent through it from the program to the file and vice versa. Lines 140-200 represent a FOR/NEXT loop in which each increment on the loop variable transfers the data to the buffer and then transfers the data from the buffer to a record in the file. Line 250 closes the file on channel 1. Line 500 ends the program.

CHAPTER 10

MATRIX OPERATIONS

A **matrix** is a rectangular array of numbers. A matrix is equivalent to use of one- and two-dimensional numeric arrays, where the first subscript refers to the number of rows and the second subscript refers to the number of columns.

The MATrix statements represent a set of BASIC instructions that greatly facilitate read, input, print, algebraic, and other matrix operations. These statements include variations from computer system to computer system. Apple II and IBM PC systems usually do not use the MATrix statements in modern BASIC languages.

10.1 MAT READ, INPUT, AND PRINT STATEMENTS

Computers having MAT READ, MAT INPUT, and MAT PRINT statements in BASIC can handle many one- and two-dimensional array problems easier than computers using multiple FOR/NEXT loops. For example,

10 MAT READ A	replaces	10 FOR R = 1 TO 3
		20 FOR C=1 TO 2
		30 READ A(R,C)
		40 NEXT C
		50 NEXT R

Similarly,

10 MAT INPUT A	replaces	10 FOR R = 1 TO 3
		20 FOR C=1 TO 2
		30 INPUT A(R,C)
		40 NEXT C
		50 NEXT R

Similarly,

10 MAT PRINT A;	replaces	10 FOR R = 1 TO 3
		20 FOR C=1 TO 2
		30 PRINT A(R,C);
		40 NEXT C
		50 NEXT R

Matrices used in BASIC require a DIM statement for one- and two-dimensional arrays. The MAT statements cannot handle all situations, however when used they can save a great deal of time and space in a program. Matrices are named in the same manner as numeric arrays. The general structure and examples of the MAT READ, INPUT, and PRINT statements are given in Table 10.1.1.

TABLE 10.1.1 MAT READ, INPUT, AND PRINT STATEMENTS

General
Structure: line no.   MAT READ list of matrix names with or
                         without explicit dimensions

line no.　MAT INPUT list of matrix names with
　　　　　or without explicit dimensions

line no.　MAT PRINT list of matrix names without
　　　　　explicit dimensions.

Examples:

Ex. 1:	10 DIM M(2,3)	Ex. 2:	10 DIM N(4,2)
	20 MAT READ M		20 MAT INPUT N
	25 MAT PRINT M;		30 MAT PRINT N:
	30 DATA		50 END
	50 END		

10.2 MATRIX FUNCTIONS

There are five common functions using MAT statements. The first two functions, ZER and CON, store a zero and one, respectively, in each element of a matrix. The general structure, meaning, and examples of each of these are given in Table 10.2.1 below.

The next three functions, IDN, TRN and INV, set up an identity matrix, transposes a matrix, and finds the inverse of a matrix, respectively. The general structure, meaning, and examples of each of these are as follows in Table 10.2.1.

TABLE 10.2.1　COMMON MATRIX FUNCTIONS

General
Structure:　line no.　MAT matrix name = ZER
　　　　　　　　　　or
　　　　　　　line no.　MAT matrix name = ZER(rows, columns)
　　　　　　　‒ ‒ ‒ ‒ ‒ ‒ ‒ ‒ ‒ ‒ ‒ ‒ ‒ ‒ ‒ ‒ ‒ ‒
　　　　　　　line no.　MAT matrix name = CON
　　　　　　　　　　or
　　　　　　　line no.　MAT matrix name = CON(rows, columns)
　　　　　　　‒ ‒ ‒ ‒ ‒ ‒ ‒ ‒ ‒ ‒ ‒ ‒ ‒ ‒ ‒ ‒ ‒ ‒

```
        line no.  MAT matrix name = IDN
                    or
        line no.  MAT matrix name = IDN(rows, columns)
— — — — — — — — — — — — — — — — — —
        line no.  MAT 1st matrix name = TRN(2nd matrix)
— — — — — — — — — — — — — — — — — —
        line no.  MAT 1st matrix name = INV(2nd matrix)
```

Examples:

Ex. 1:   10 MAT A = ZER
Ex. 2:   10 MAT Y = CON(R,C)
Ex. 3:   10 MAT Z = IDN
Ex. 4:   10 MAT A = TRN(B)
Ex. 5:   10 MAT C = INV(D)

10.3 MATRIX ALGEBRAIC OPERATIONS

The matrix functions given in Section 10.2 can be used in combination with certain algebraic operations. The basic operations are: addition/subtraction, assignment, scalar multiplication, and matrix multiplication. The general structure and examples for these operations are given in Table 10.3.1.

TABLE 10.3.1 MATRIX ALGEBRAIC OPERATIONS

General
Structure: line no. MAT first matrix = second matrix

    line no. MAT 1st matrix = 2nd matrix + 3rd mat
    line no. MAT 1st matrix = 2nd matrix − 3rd mat

    line no. MAT 1st matrix=(expression)∗ 2nd mat

    line no. MAT 1st matrix=2nd matrix ∗ 2nd mat

Examples:

Ex. 1:   10 MAT A = B
Ex. 2:   20 MAT B = C + D
Ex. 3:   25 MAT B = C − D
Ex. 4:   30 MAT X = (4)∗A
Ex. 5:   40 MAT Y = A∗B

MATrix Operation Rule 1: All matrices must be the same dimension if they are added or subtracted in BASIC.

MATrix Operation Rule 2: For matrix multiplication, the number of columns in the first matrix must equal the number of rows in the second matrix, and the number of rows in the first matrix must equal the number of columns in the second matrix.

MATrix Operation Rule 3: In the inverse matrix operation (e.g., 10 MAT A = INV(B), the two matrices involved must be square matrices and have the same dimension.

10.4 SOME COMMON ERRORS

(A)   If the DIM statement of an array is omitted when using a MAT statement, then an error may occur the first time the MAT statement is used in the program.

(B)   The ZER, CON, and IDN are the only MAT statements that can be redimensioned during the execution of the MAT READ and MAT INPUT statements in a program.

(C) Some functions and operations may not allow the same matrix to appear on both sides of the equal sign.

10.5 DEMONSTRATION PROGRAM

```
100 CLS
102 REM * PROGRAM LOADS AND PRINTS *
104 REM * TWO MATRICES              *
105 DIM A(2,2), B(2,2)
107 FOR R=1 TO 2                      Replacements for IBM
108 FOR C=1 TO 2                      and Apple II computers
109 REM *READ AND PRINT STATEMENTS*
110 MAT READ A(R,C), B(R,C)           110 READ A(R,C), B(R,C)
120 MAT PRINT A(R,C);                 120 PRINT A(R,C);
140 MAT PRINT B(R,C)                  140 PRINT B(R,C)
172 NEXT C
174 NEXT R
180 DATA 20, 10, 15, 30
190 DATA 17, 24, 29, 40
200 END
```

Lines 100-105 clear the screen, describe the program and reserve two 2-dimensional arrays in memory. Lines 107-174 are two nested FOR/NEXT loops in which values for the two matrices are read from the DATA lines, stored, and the results printed. Lines 180 and 190 are not executed. Line 200 is the end of the program.

The replacement statements for lines 110-140 will allow the user to run the program on an Apple II or IBM PC system.

110

CHAPTER 11

STRING FUNCTIONS

The ability to process strings of characters is an essential part of extended BASIC. In BASIC, string expressions include string constants, string variables, string function references, and a combination of these separated by the concatenation operator (+). This section includes some of the common string functions.

11.1 THE LEFT$, LEN, MID$ AND RIGHT$ STRING FUNCTIONS

Concatenation is the only valid string operation. However, the LEFT$, LEN, MID$ and RIGHT$ string functions allow for some additional manipulation. These functions are defined in Table 11.1.1 below.

TABLE 11.1.1 DEFINITIONS OF THE LEFT$, LEN, MID$ AND RIGHT$ STRING FUNCTIONS

Function	Function Definition
LEFT$(X$,N)	Extracts the leftmost N characters of the string X$

LEN(X$)	Determines the length of the string X$ and returns a positive integer value
MID$(X$,P,N)	Extracts N characters of the string X$ starting at position P
RIGHT$(X$,N)	Extracts the rightmost N characters of the string X$

(**Note:** X$ is a string expression and N and P are numeric expressions.)

Table 11.1.2 gives the general structure and examples of the four string functions defined in Table 11.1.1. The BASIC language for both Apple and IBM PC BASIC utilizes these functions.

TABLE 11.1.2 THE LEFT$, LEN, MID$ AND RIGHT$ FUNCTIONS

General
Structure: line no.   String variable = LEFT$(X$, N)
             line no.   Variable = LEN(X$)
             line no.   String variable = MID$(X$, P, N)
             line no.   String variable = RIGHT$(X$, N)

Examples:

Ex. 1:   10 A$ = LEFT$(X$, 8)
Ex. 2:   20 B$ = LEN(X$)
Ex. 3:   30 C$ = MID$(X$, 4, 20)
Ex. 4:   40 D$ = RIGHT$(X$, 12)

Note: X$ = "IS BASIC FOR BEGINNERS AND EXPERTS?"

11.2 FUNCTIONS FOR CONVERTING CHARACTER CODES AND MODIFYING DATA TYPES

The ASC and CHR$ functions are used to convert character codes while STR$ and VAL functions are used to modify data types. The definitions of these functions are given in Table 11.2.1.

TABLE 11.2.1 DEFINITION OF FUNCTIONS FOR CONVERTING CHARACTER CODES AND MODIFYING DATA TYPES

Function	Function Definition
ASC(C$)	Produces a two-digit value equivalent in ASCII code to the single character C$.
CHR$(N)	Produces a single string character equivalent in ASCII code to the numeric argument N.
STR$(N)	Produces the string equivalent of the numeric argument N.
VAL(X$)	Produces the numeric equivalent of the string argument X$.

The general structure and examples of the character code functions, and functions to modify data types, are given in Table 11.2.2. These functions are common for both the Apple and IBM PC.

TABLE 11.2.2   THE ASC AND CHR$ FUNCTIONS

General
Structure: line no.   Numeric Variable = ASC(C$)
line no.   String Variable = CHR$(N)
line no.   String Variable = STR$(N)
line no.   Numeric Variable = VAL(X$)

Examples:

Ex. 1:   10 A = ASC("5")
Ex. 2:   20 D$ = CHR$(4)
Ex. 3:   30 B$ = STR$(34)
Ex. 4:   40 C = VAL ("3.14")

11.3 OTHER ENHANCED BASIC STRING FUNCTIONS

There are a number of other enhanced BASIC string functions, such as the DATE$, TIME$, INKEY$ (GET X$), INPUT$(N), SPACE$(N), SPC(N), INSTR(P,X$,S$), and STRING$(N,"C") functions, which are not covered in this chapter. Consult the BASIC manual for your computer system for details concerning their definitions and general structures. Some of these functions are not a part of both Apple and IBM PC BASIC systems.

11.4 SOME COMMON ERRORS

(A)   Failure to remember the different data type forms may cause unexpected results when using string functions.

(B)   Failure to follow exactly the structure of a string function usually leads to an error that is difficult to correctly debug if several string functions are being used in a program.

11.5 DEMONSTRATION PROGRAMS

```
100 CLS
105 REM ** STRING MANIPULATION **
110 S$ = "ESSENTIALS OF BASIC"
120 PRINT S$
130 PRINT MID$(S$,6, 10)
140 PRINT
145 REM ** ASCII CONVERSION **
150 INPUT "ENTER ANY CHARACTER ";C$
160 LET A = ASC(C$)
170 PRINT "THE ASCII VALUE OF '";C$;"' IS ";A
175 PRINT
180 PRINT "NOW WE CONVERT BACK TO THE CHARACTER ENTERED"
190 PRINT "THE CHARACTER ENTERED WAS: ";CHR$(A)
192 PRINT
193 LET L = LEN(S$)
195 PRINT "THE LENGTH OF THE ORIGINAL STATEMENT IS "
197 PRINT L;" CHARACTERS."
200 END
```

Lines 100-105 clear the screen and describe the program. Lines 110-140 assign a string to S$, print it, print 10 characters of S$ starting with the character in the 6th position from the left, and skip a line. Lines 150-192 accept a character; change it in line 160 to its ASCII code number; print the original character and its code; skip a single line; print a label; convert the ASCII back to the original character; and skip a single line. Lines 193-197 calculate and print the length of the original string S$.

```
100 HOME
105 REM ** PROGRAM COMMENTS: **
110 REM ** LINE NUMBER 150 CENTERS THE A$. **
112 REM ** OTHER LINE NUMBERS DEMONSTRATE THE LEFT$, **
115 REM ** RIGHT$, LEN AND MID$ STATEMENTS. **
120 INPUT A$
130 PRINT A$
140 PRINT
150 PRINT TAB((40 - LEN(A$))/2 + 1); A$
165 LET A$ = "TENNIS"
170 LET B$ = LEFT$(A$,3)
180 LET C$ = MID$(A$, 2, 3)
190 LET D$ = RIGHT$(A$, 2)
200 PRINT B$, C$, D$
500 END
```

Lines 100-115 clear the screen and describe the program. Lines 120-160 accept and print a string, printing the string centered on a 40-column line. Lines 165-200 assign "Tennis" to A$, assign the left three characters of A$ to B$, assign the middle three characters of A$ (starting with the letter e) to C$, assign the last two characters of A$ to D$, and print all three assigned variables. Line 500 is the end of the program.

APPENDIX A

COMMON SYSTEM FEATURES

COMMON BASIC SYSTEM COMMANDS

When writing BASIC programs some system commands are necessary. This appendix gives a summary of these for both the Apple and IBM PC.

Command	Apple Computer
[Note: <RETURN> key must be pressed after typed statement.]	
List	Type LIST
Execute	Type RUN
Delete a line	Type line #
Save a program on a disk	Type SAVE program name
Load a program from a disk	Type LOAD program name
Clear memory for a new program	Type NEW
Display disk directory	Type CATALOG

117

Delete a file	Type DELETE filename
Initialize a disk	Type INIT HELLO
Lock a file	Type LOCK filename
Unlock a file	Type UNLOCK filename
Activate 80-column mode	Type PR#3
Rename a file	Type RENAME <old file>, <new file>

Command	IBM PC

[Note: <ENTER> key must be pressed after typed statement.]

List	Type LIST
Execute	Type RUN
Delete a line	Type DELETE line #
Save a program to a disk	Type SAVE"<disk drive>: program name"
Load a program from a disk	Type LOAD"<disk drive>: program name"
Delete a file from a disk	Type KILL"<disk drive>: program name"
Clear memory for a new program	Type NEW

118

Display directory of a disk	Type FILES (for Drive A)
	   or FILES"B:*.*"
	  or
	Type DIR <disk drive>

Renumber line of a program	Type RENUMBER <newline>, <startline>, <increment>
Merge program on disk with one in memory	Type MERGE"<program name>"
Rename a file or program	Type RENAME <old name> <new name>
Leave DOS to enter BASIC	Type BASIC or BASICA
Leave BASIC to enter DOS	Type SYSTEM
Duplicate a file or program	Type COPY <original>
Format a new disk	Type FORMAT <disk drive>
Copy an entire disk	Type DISKCOPY <original disk>: <backup>

CLEAR SCREEN PROCEDURES AND HARD COPY OUTPUT

CLEAR SCREEN PROCEDURES

For the Apple the HOME statement within a program clears the screen and places the cursor in the upper left hand corner of the screen. The same statement may be used to clear the screen in the immediate mode (without being a part of a program).

For the IBM PC the CLS statement within a program clears the screen and places the cursor in the upper left hand corner of the screen. The same statement may be used to clear the screen in the immediate mode (without being a part of a program).

HARD COPY OUTPUT

For the Apple, PR#1 activates the printer while PR#0 deactivates the printer. To obtain a hard copy of a program in the computer's memory and its output results, do the following:

Type PR#1 then press <RETURN>
Type LIST then press <RETURN>

Type RUN then press <RETURN>
Type PR#0 then press <RETURN>

For the IBM PC, to get a hard copy listing of a program in memory simply type LLIST and press the ENTER key. To get a listing of the program and its output results, do the following:

Simultaneously press the CTRL and Prt Sc keys
Type LLIST then press <ENTER>
Type RUN then press <ENTER>
Simultaneously press the CTRL and Prt Sc keys